Illustrated by Alphonse Tvaryanas

Photography by:
  Island School of Underwater Photography,
    Red Hook, St. Thomas, U.S.V.I.
  Dan Nerney — photos pp. 8-9, 12, 16, 36, 38-39,
    62-63, 64, 67, 74, 88-89, 91, 100-101, 105
    (bottom), 107, 119, 128, 132-133, 136, 141 (top), 143
    (top), 144-145, 149, 151, 152, 153, 160-161, 170-171,
    190-191, 216
  Edward Stevenson — photos pp. 4, 14, 20, 26, 42, 50,
    59, 212-213.

Thanks to Navtec, Inc. for the illustration, p. 142, and
to The Cordage Institute, Loos & Co., Inc., and J. Stuart Haft Co. for the tables reproduced in the appendix.
A special word of appreciation to John "Scotty" Mac-
Donald of MacDonald Yacht Rigging, Inc., Stamford,
C.T., and to Sonja Douglas for her invaluable guidance
in the production of this book.

© Tree Communications Inc 1979, 1982

First published in the United States of America by
Bobbs-Merrill Company Inc., New York/Indianapolis

British Library Cataloguing in Publication Data
MacLean, William P.
  Modern marlinspike seamanship: knots, splices,
  cordage, terminals and rigging.
  1. Knots and splices
  2. Marlinspike seamanship
  I. Title
  623.88″82   VN531

ISBN 0-7153-8328-0

Printed in Great Britain by Butler & Tanner Ltd, Frome,
for David & Charles (Publishers) Limited
Brunel House Newton Abbot Devon

Contents

Preface

This book is written as a popular guide to ropes, cables, chain, and other materials used under tension. Yachtsmen, and especially sailors, being more involved with marlinspike than anyone else, are the primary audience I address. Much of the information could also be useful to mountaineers, general contractors, and others who use cordage. My goal is to make the pertinent engineering principles accessible to yachtsmen and others who have long relied on conventional wisdom and tradition. My experience as a teacher and a popularizer of science is that the greatest obstacle in such an effort is convincing the audience that understanding is possible and that great intellectual effort is not required. I am delighted now to be able to write for yachtsmen, who, because they pursue one of the most technological sports, already have been exposed to vectors and calculations.

I fall into neither of the classic categories of yachting authors. I am not an engineer or designer who has spent a career advancing nautical technology, nor am I an old salt who rounded the Horn on square riggers (or any other kind of craft). I am an ecology professor who has sailed several thousand miles and who has owned three yachts.

A brief review of the genesis of this book will enable me to acknowledge the many people who helped. My wife, Ellen, and I moved to the Virgin Islands 10 years ago partly to do more sailing. After owning two smaller cruisers, EEYORE and IPHISA, we decided to build our ultimate yacht, CYC-LURA. I spent a few years planning and selecting the design and designer. I inspected a sister ship, S. R. Averich's boat, and I pestered Jerry Cartwright, the designer, before making the selection—Cartwright 40. Jerry, his charming wife, Kay, and S. R. have become friends and have helped me with both the boat and book projects. I was especially fortunate in being able to examine many of the competitors in the last OSTAR race with Jerry; no weakness in a yacht escapes his criticism.

By the time I reached the stage of making lists of lists for the boat project, I also managed to just afford really going ahead. Jerry steered me towards the yard which owned a hull mold for his 40-footer, New England Boat Builders. I signed a contract with NEBB to build a hull and to install bulkheads, engine, deck, cabin sole, and chainplates. The project worked out very well for all concerned. The boat was launched after Ellen and I spent three hard months installing electrics, deck hardware, and a minimal interior. In another three weeks, I had her completely rigged and commissioned. We did a few shakedown sails across Buzzard's Bay, and were on our way home, across the open Atlantic, in less than four weeks after launching. We spent only very slightly more money than we had, which in yachting is miraculous. The owner of the yard, John Deroce, was incredibly tolerant, letting me work along with his crew. He and Joan, his wife, were also very cordial to us, frequently feeding us a much-needed hearty meal. Allan Vaitses, the manager and former owner of NEBB, reasonably and cheerfully answered questions at a rate of several per hour for months. He well deserves his fame as the reigning master of the scientific art of building yachts. Everett, Bill, Lightning, Whitey, and John were very helpful and became good friends. I would gladly sell CYCLURA, just to be able to go back and build another Cartwright 40 at NEBB. Other friends in Massachusetts, the Briggs, the Boudreaus, the Rileys, and Peter Ellen among them, helped the CYCLURA project along. Charlie Shabica came from Chicago

to work for a week, and Adele Jenney lent us a car and helped in many other ways. Some distinguished yachtsmen, such as Hal Roth, passed through, took a look, and offered very useful suggestions.

Professor Stanley Backer of MIT gave me an invaluable lecture on the mechanics of cordage and structure. Several of my colleagues at the College of the Virgin Islands have helped me with technical questions.

I dwell on the building of CYCLURA because it became intermingled with the writing of this book. Bruce Michel suggested that I write a knot book in December 1976 and from then on, all analysis that went into CYCLURA's rigging was also considered in a more general context. While in New England, Ellen and I made the rounds of the major rope manufacturers, Samson, New England, and Yale Cordage, who received us graciously but did not show us around their plants. We spent hours talking to Dave Biddle and Frank Colinari of Bay Sailing Equipment in Fall River. Ken King of Navtec gave us a tour and answered questions.

Continuing my research after launching CYCLURA, I was helped by William and Alfred Carranza of Sunshine Cordage, Donald Gilluley from Gladding, H. E. W. Van Stijn of Hivas Nederland, Carl Moser of Loos and Co., Dick Knights of Marlow Ropes Ltd., and Lee Ward, the manufacturer of STA-LOK terminals. I have talked to many yachtsmen. My friend Yvonne van der Byl, skipper of SAYULA II, has been especially helpful. Skip Michel, president of Sailors' World Ships' Store, has contributed to every stage of the building of CYCLURA and of the writing of this book, as has his charming wife, Loesje. Skip and I have argued many of the fine points and have often reached an agreement. The result is much improved.

Introduction

Yachting is a technical sport. One cannot dock a powerboat or track a sailboat without solving, intuitively or analytically, some basic engineering problems. Having mastered the basic kinds of problems, yachtsmen move on to more complex topics, such as navigation, racing tactics, tuning of rigging, and sail trimming. Many yachtsmen do everything themselves and a few even design or build their own boats.

Marlinspike seamanship is one of the technical specialties which the yachtsman must master. It includes knots, splices, and, according to my conception, everything to do with rigging, ropes, and chains on boats. On sailboats, marlinspike occupies a great deal of one's attention, because there is so much of it. On powerboats, there is no standing or running rigging (with a few minor exceptions), but marlinspike knowledge is still required for dealing with dock lines, anchor rodes, and davits.

Marlinspike encompasses some of the oldest human technology — a number of the standard knots have prehistoric origins. During the great age of sail, marlinspike practice reached its peak of development, partly due to the extent and complexity of rigging on square riggers, but also because sailors needed a pastime on long ocean voyages which, in the case of whalers, could last years.

Modern marlinspike practice is just now coming into its own. Many of the materials used are relatively new and traditions give way only slowly to new developments. This is especially evident in the currently available literature on marlinspike, which is made up partly of reprints of outdated classic works and partly of new books with decidedly nostalgic tones. Yachting magazines have done a good job of keeping up with the developments, but articles vary widely in quality and do not necessarily remain available. (In fact, I had to obtain one article, less than two years old, from the Library of Congress.)

When I started to write this book, I soon realized two things: that knots are not used very frequently on modern yachts, and that marlinspike now includes a great deal more than knots and splices. Walking along docks in marinas, I have counted numbers of actual knots in use on individual boats. I find that observable knots average fewer than six per boat and that it is not uncommon to see none at all — splices are more common these days. The modern marlinspike sailor is spending his time working on terminals, turnbuckles, shackles, and other hardware, which have replaced shroud eyes, deadeyes, and lanyards, and most splices, knots, lashings, and seizings. Unfortunately, this new focus has led to a decline in yachtsmen's skill in making the knots and splices which *are* still quite useful.

This book defines what I think marlinspike seamanship has become and what the yachtsman needs to know to be self-sufficient. I have attempted to derive as much as possible from basic engineering principles and to compare alternative ways of doing things. It could have been much longer or shorter, or more or less technical, but the present length and level appear to suit the topic and the audience. I learned as much about yachts by writing it as I did by building CYCLURA.

**Chapter 1
Knots**

It is difficult to define the term knot very concisely or with much precision — the word has always been used rather loosely. In dictionary terms, a knot is an interweaving of the parts of one or more ropes, cords, or the like, made for the purpose of fastening them together or to something else, or to prevent the end of a rope, etc. from passing through a hole, sheave, or block. Bends are a special class of knots used specifically for fastening or "bending" ropes together end-to-end. Hitches are another special group of knots, used principally to fasten a rope or line to an object such as a post, spar, stanchion, or other line.

We can make a further functional division between plain or working knots — those used primarily for their mechanical properties — and fancy knots which are used primarily because of their appearance. The present chapter concerns the plain or working knots — the relatively simple ties that are indispensable as mechanical devices on shipboard. Several books are available which catalogue and describe knots exhaustively. Researchers, drawing mainly from the complex technology of nineteenth century square-rigged sailing, have been able to find several thousand different knots. My purpose here is different. I will identify and discuss the relatively small number of knots which it is essential to know in covering the situations that arise on modern yachts. First, however, I would like to offer some comments on the subject of knot strength.

Strength of Knots

Knots have one big advantage over splices and other methods of joining and fastening ropes: they can be rapidly and easily tied and untied. The disadvantage of knots is that they significantly weaken the ropes in which they are tied. Thus knots should never be considered anything more than a temporary means of attaching or uniting ropes and lines, except in very low-stress situations.

Many sailors think that the strength of knots is their resistance to untying — if the correct knot has been selected for the job and has been properly tied, it will not untie itself. The so-called strength of knots might be better expressed in negative terms — the weakness of knots relative to the ropes in which they are tied.

All knots have a "nip" (or more than one), the part of the rope which is arranged so as to grab, squeeze, or jam against another part. Nips all wrap around the parts they grab or pinch, causing the rope to turn about very tight radii. Tight turns always result in significantly uneven loading of fibers, because the fibers on the outside of the turn travel much farther than those on the inside.

Consideration of a simple model, the overhand knot, should clarify this. Imagine a length of rope with parallel lines running its length. When tied in an overhand knot, this imaginary rope maintains its circular cross section and stretches to accommodate the geometry of the knot. It is easy to see that the lateral line that travels the greatest distance through the knot (around the outside) is much longer than the shortest (inside) line — almost three times as long, in fact (see figure A).

In other words, crimping a rope into a tight bend of any kind will cause great stretching around the outside of the bend and consider-

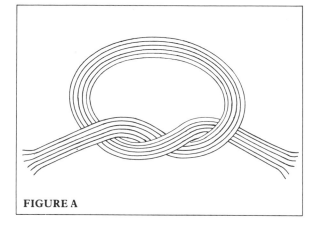

FIGURE A

able compression at the inside, even though the fibers in a real rope behave quite differently from the parallel lines in our imaginary model. (The real fibers do not run parallel along the length of the line, nor are they perfectly elastic as we postulated our imaginary rope to be.) In a real rope the fibers shift or migrate within the larger components, and the whole rope changes shape (flattens) to accommodate the tension as much as possible, but the result is still very uneven loading of the structure as a whole.

Due to the complexities of the mechanical relationships involved, it is virtually impossible to make a strictly accurate engineering analysis of all the factors affecting knot strength. If we can understand the general principles of what is happening within a knot, however, we will have some broad guidelines on what to expect from various kinds of knots in various types of ropes.

Fiber elasticity is probably the most important factor influencing knot strength. A very elastic fiber under load will elongate so that part of the load will then be transferred to other fibers which were initially unloaded. If the fibers are not elastic, the first fibers to bear the load will break before any of the load can be transferred to other fibers. Nylon

ropes should thus make the strongest knots. Other ropes should have knot strengths roughly proportional to their elasticity.

The geometry of fibers in a rope can also be expected to affect the strength of knots. The fibers in twisted ropes have considerable freedom to migrate, changing the rope's shape to accommodate the uneven tension; the fibers in the sheath of double braid are much more restricted in their ability to move. The kind of sharp-bend load we are talking about here should be more evenly distributed among the fibers of the twisted rope, all other things being equal. For the same reason, greater knot strength should be expected in a soft-lay rope than in a hard rope.

All knots are weak, some more than others. Knots such as the bowline and clove hitch are popular because they are relatively strong, due to the way the nip is distributed. The bowline, for example, is frequently said to be 60 percent as strong as the line it is tied in. The user should be aware, however, that this is an optimum figure — depending on the type of line in question, the bowline may weaken it to as little as 10 percent of its unknotted breaking strength. The only knot described in this chapter that is particularly noteworthy for its weakness is the sheepshank; it should be used only as a temporary expedient and never under a large load. Knots should be replaced with splices in any remotely permanent arrangement. The accidental overhand and other knots that tend to appear in dinghy painters and other lines should be promptly untied.

Figure Eight Knot

There are many situations where it is useful to have a knot in the end of a rope so that it cannot fit through a block or cleat. Such stopper knots are routinely used to prevent the loss of halyards and sheets on sailboats. They are also useful on the ends of dinghy davits and other tackles, and on dock and anchor lines. A stopper knot is easier to grip than a plain rope end, and one can be quickly made in an end which must be pulled, such as a dock line which does not quite reach

a cleat. (A stopper knot can also be used as a temporary means of preventing a cut or chafed rope end from unravelling, but knotting is not a satisfactory permanent substitute for whipping.) The figure eight knot is the standard stopper knot and, in many ways, the best. It is easily tied and untied and it increases rope diameter by a factor of three. There are other stopper knots better suited for some special situations, but the figure eight knot is the workhorse.

1. Make a bight in the end of the rope, passing the end under the standing part.

2. Pass the end over the near side and through the loop.

3. The knot drawn up. A quick way to tie the figure eight is to go through the motions of tying a simple overhand loop, but giving the bight a half twist before putting the tail through the loop.

Ashley's Stopper Knot

This knot was invented by Clifford W. Ashley, the greatest student of knots and splices in our century. He called it the "Oysterman's stopper knot." It is easily tied and untied and is larger than the figure eight, making it more suited to certain special situations.

Ashley's story about the invention and naming of this stopper knot is that he saw a curious knot on the end of a halyard on a passing Chesapeake oystering ketch. The knot was larger than the usual figure eight, and he tried to duplicate it. After a while he

came up with his stopper. Later at a dock, he was able to examine the halyard end carefully, only to discover that what he had seen was a figure eight tied on a particularly long-jawed and frayed rope end. This apparently suggested to him that other knots of general usefulness could still be invented, in spite of several thousand years' accumulation of forms. Ashley did go on to invent several other knots, including the constrictor knot which I describe later. These two knots of Ashley's illustrate that the best inventions are usually quite simple.

14

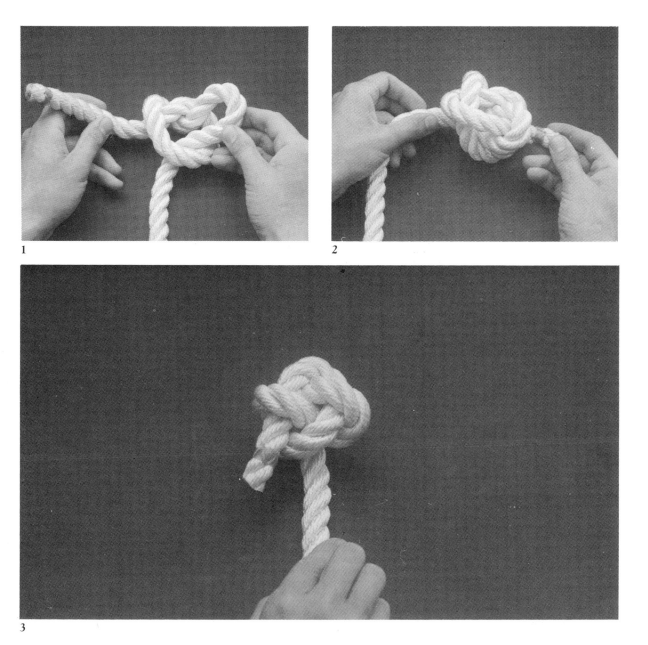

1   2

3

1. A delightfully simple and ingenious knot. A simple loop is made with the standing part passing over the end. The standing part is then pulled up through the loop forming a bight.

2. The end is passed through the bight.

3. The knot must be carefully drawn up.

Reef Knot

This knot, called the "square knot" by Boy Scouts and nonseafarers, is used in its double-slipped form to tie shoelaces. On boats, it is used to tie reefs into sails (hence its name) and for many other comparable purposes like lacing sail covers and lashings. It is the best knot for these applications.

Unfortunately, the reef knot is so much more widely known than any other knot that its misuse is frequent. It should never be used to bend two ropes together, for instance. It has two very serious shortcomings as a bend: it either capsizes into two half hitches and a straight end or, if it holds, it tightens and becomes almost impossible to untie. In some cases, the failure of a reef knot under load could be a serious matter — I certainly would not want to be around if this happened with nylon towlines.

The reef knot is frequently mistied as well as misapplied. The incorrect form is called the "granny knot" — more than nonfunctional, it is a downright dangerous knot which should be avoided because it unties itself. The process of tying the reef knot correctly involves making two overhand knots that are mirror images of each other. Right over left followed by left over right results in the reef knot, whereas right over left and then right over left again results in the granny. Properly tied, the reef knot takes the form of two interlocked loops.

1. A simple overhand knot.

2. Followed by a mirror-image overhand. The hands must make opposite motions in tying the two halves of the knot. It is easy to tell by observation of the distinctive geometry of the knot—two loops threaded through each other—whether you have tied it correctly, but every sailor should have this knot, like the bowline, in his fingers.

1

2

GRANNY KNOT

Granny knot, the infamous "wrong form" of the reef knot; it slips, capsizes, and jams. It results when the hands follow the same sequence of motions in tying both halves of the reef knot.

Clove Hitch

This knot presents a tying problem similar to that of the reef knot. So many people find these knots difficult to master that I am not convinced there is any easy solution to the difficulty. With practice, anyone should be able to overcome knot-tying difficulties; I think that being able to visualize the outcome is invaluable. The clove hitch has an elegantly simple geometry that, once visualized, is imprinted on the mind and difficult to mistie.

This knot is used to attach a line to a rigid column, be it a spar, piling, or lifeline. The rope rounds the column twice in the same direction and the two standing parts are nipped beneath the part connecting the two full loops. The two ends do not cross one another.

If pull on the standing part of the rope can take many directions, it is better to use a rolling hitch, because the clove hitch can roll around a column and untie itself. The standing end of a clove hitch should not be allowed to turn around the nip, as this tends to loosen the knot.

The clove hitch, properly tied, is very good for attaching dock lines to pilings; bowlines used for this purpose tend to chafe. Other common uses of this knot are hanging bumpers from lifelines, tying halyards and awnings to standing rigging, attaching dinghy painters to stanchions, and tying off tillers and wheels. Clove hitches become very difficult to untie if subjected to long and heavy loading, however, especially when tied on small-diameter columns. This makes this knot unsuitable for attaching anchor and towlines to Samson posts and other similar uses. The tugman's hitch is much better for this, since it can be set free even when loaded.

1. A loop is made.

2. Another loop is laid on top with the standing part running opposite to the free end.

3. The two loops are slipped over the end of the spar, etc., and the hitch is drawn tight by pulling on the ends. An easy method of tying the clove hitch over an object where it is not possible to slip it over the end: Loop the rope over the spar once. Cross the end over the standing part. Make a second full loop and pass the end under the top of the second loop where it crosses over. Draw tight.

1

2

3

Tugman's Hitch

This knot is invaluable for tying down a line under load to a post or winch. Many other knots and tangles of rope are used for this purpose, but no other really has the tugman's hitch's fine qualities of ease of tying and of release.

Virtually every yachtsman eventually accepts a tow. Many towing calamities result from not being able to throw the towline off quickly. For this reason alone, every yachtsman should know this knot. It will also prove useful in many other situations, such as when a sheet cleat rips out or breaks. I use this knot for attaching lines to the drum of CYCLURA's windlass, and I once had to use it on sheet winches: CYCLURA was far from sorted out when we made a 12-day passage home, four weeks after her launching. She has no sheet cleats, only self-tailing winches, which work well as long as the sheets are of the right size. Some of the sheets were oversize and had to be tied to the winches with this knot.

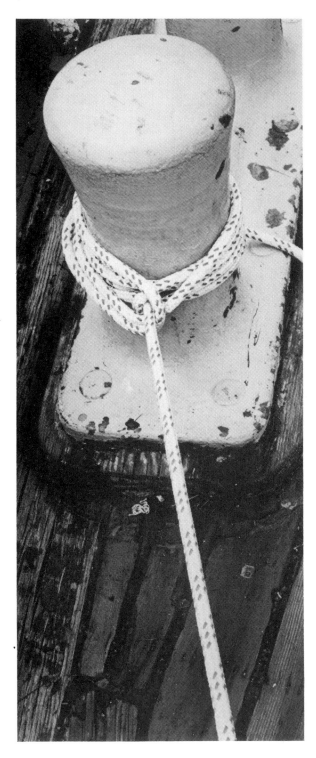

1. A tugman's hitch is used to belay on a post or
drum, especially when it might be necessary to cast
off under heavy load. The first step is to take several
turns. Then pass a loop under the standing part and
over the drum.

2. After a wrap around the drum in the opposite
direction, pass another loop under the standing part
and put this over as well.

3. The hitch completed. This very useful procedure
is not widely known.

Rolling Hitch

This handy knot has fallen into general disuse, which I attribute to its name and the typical illustration of its use: towing a pole or log. In a small pamphlet given away by The Cordage Group it is called the "taut-line hitch" and is shown as a means of transferring the load from one line to another — an application more pertinent to the yachtsman. I first learned this knot to earn a merit badge in the Boy Scouts, but only years later, while reading about the handling of anchor tackle in the sixteenth century, did I realize its best application. Anchor rodes used to be of immense diameter, up to 10 or 12 inches, in the days when natural-fiber ropes were used on ships. We have all seen the use of a capstan in the movies, but the actual method of operation is rarely shown or explained. As the rode was far too large to be wrapped around a capstan drum, a continuous line was used to transfer the load. This line took several turns around the drum and was then attached to the rode by rope tails which were tied onto the rode with rolling hitches and untied as they went slack, the load being transferred to tails tied farther down the rode. As anchoring was more frequent in the days of sail, when much time was spent waiting for fair tides and winds, the rolling hitch might well have been the most frequently used knot.

Today, the rolling hitch is still very useful for transferring the load off one rope onto another. It is invaluable in handling ground tackle. Handling anchors off the stern is usually difficult due to obstructions and the lack of a roller. A rode can be payed out from the bow and then transferred to the stern with a smaller line bent onto the rode with this knot. All possible methods which do not

use a second line result in the rode going slack for a time, which makes it hard getting to a dock bow-to. I can dock CYCLURA single-handed this way, as long as I do not have to counter substantial wind or tide on the beam.

Spring lines can be attached to rope or chain rodes using rolling hitches. This is a good way to take the load off the windlass and to stop bow rollers from squeaking. The spring lines can be small enough to lead through bow chocks and cleat down, while the rode might not be. This is a good method of reducing chafe on nylon rodes.

The rolling hitch also provides the best means of getting riding turns off winches. A tag line is bent onto the jammed sheet and the load taken up on another winch. If no other winch is convenient, a tackle or handy-billy can be used. This method is also useful to get around having too few winches, such as when both spinnaker and genoa are up on a boat with no secondary cockpit winches.

If a chafed line is likely to fail or if a line might come off its cleat or winch, a safety line can be attached with a rolling hitch.

1

4

2

1. To start a rolling hitch, wrap the rope twice around the chain, rope, etc., on which it is being tied.

2. Then bring the end across the standing part.

3. Finish off with a half hitch.

4. The completed hitch. This knot is invaluable in transferring strain from one rope to another. Applications include removing riding turns from a winch, hauling an anchor rode with cockpit winches, and making an adjustable loop by tying the rolling hitch on the standing part of the same rope.

3

Bowline

This is the most versatile knot aboard ship and almost everywhere else. It is the best knot for putting a fixed loop in the end of a rope because it never slips or unties itself, yet it is easily untied regardless of the load it has carried. Bowlines cannot be untied under load, however, so they should not be used where this will be necessary, such as in towlines or sheets and halyards at their free ends. The only other limitation of the bowline applies to all knots, and that is that it is weaker than the rope it is tied in. In any application where a loop can be left in place permanently, an eye splice, which is as strong as the rope if properly done, should be used instead of a knot.

The applications of the bowline are numerous and for the most part, obvious. I will merely mention a few general cases. The major use of bowlines is to make a loop which will be placed over a piling, cleat, or other solid object after it has been tied.

Bowlines can also be tied with the loop already in place around a high piling, for example, or through a ring.

The bowline is the basis of some satisfactory methods of bending ropes together. Two lines can be joined by interlocking bowlines, or a sheet bend can be tied onto the loop of a bowline. The major disadvantage of these methods over a carrick bend or simple sheet bend is that more rope is used. The bends, however, are weaker than a bowline; the double bowline method may be the strongest way of joining lines, short of splicing.

It is conventional to tie the bowline so that the free rope end is inside the loop. Hervey Garrett Smith calls this the right-handed bowline and claims that it is far superior to the left-handed bowline, with the end outside of the loop. I cannot confirm this, but I would be happier if everyone could tie some kind of bowline. The number of sailors who cannot make a bowline at all is disgraceful.

1

4

2

1. Set the loop size for a bowline.

2. Pass the end through the loop. Note that the end and the standing part are on opposing sides of the loop. There are more rapid ways of tying bowlines, but this step-by-step method should be mastered first.

3. Bring the end around the standing part. Then bring the end back through the loop.

4. The completed bowline. Draw up the knot by pulling on the end and loop with one hand, and the standing part with the other. With heavy ropes, it will be necessary to work the loops into shape to tighten the knot properly.

3

Sheet Bend

This is the most versatile bend or means of joining two ropes end-to-end. It is the best bend for small, supple, or slippery ropes and works well in almost all situations, except when two large, stiff ropes are to be connected, in which case the carrick bend is best. (Large, stiff ropes make it impossible to draw a sheet up tight by hand. It may untie under load as a result. The carrick bend, however, draws itself up nicely.)

The sheet bend is the only suitable knot for tying onto a rope end with an eye splice. It is frequently used to extend dock lines for this reason. As the sheet bend is geometrically identical to the bowline, differing only in that it joins two lines instead of making a loop, it is easily untied regardless of the load it has endured.

Unlike most American yachts, which use bowlines to attach separate sheets to jib

clews, CYCLURA has one-part sheets with a seized eye in the middle, through which a tag line from the clew is attached with a sheet bend. The tag line, which is smaller rope than the sheets (⅜-inch and ½-inch respectively) is tied through the clew with a bowline on a bight, and both of its ends are used in the sheet bend. The advantages of this arrangement are, first, that all of the clew chafe is on the tag line, which can be easily and inexpensively replaced and, second, that there is only one knot to tie when sails are changed or reefed. The reefing clews also have tag lines which are left on permanently; on the staysail the tag line is long enough to get the sheets aft of the forward lower shrouds, where chafe is likely to occur. I use a double sheet bend in all of these situations, because it is easier to untie than the single sheet bend.

1

2

3

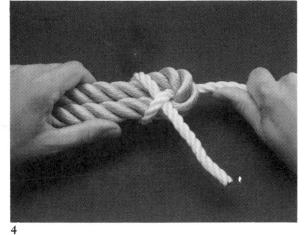

4

5

1. Starting a sheet bend. Form a loop in the larger rope and pass the end of the smaller rope through it.

2. Wrap the end of the smaller rope around the loop.

3. Then pass the end under its own standing part.

4. Sheet bends must be carefully drawn up or they capsize. Hold the loop in one hand, and with the other, pull alternately on the end and standing parts of the smaller rope.

5. To make a double sheet bend, carry the end around the loop another time and pass it under again. The second turn makes a much more permanent knot. Note that the sheet bend is just a bowline tied between different ropes.

Carrick Bend

Before tightening, the carrick bend is a most elegant knot, used for artistic effect on the cover of this book. Once tightened, however, its appearance suffers considerably. I have taught people to tie carrick bends and have noticed that they find the final result disappointing after the beauty of the intermediate steps. Handsome or not, the carrick bend is an elegant knot because it tightens itself under load without capsizing. This feature makes it invaluable in bending together large or stiff ropes which cannot be properly drawn up in a sheet bend or paired bowlines. There is some possibility of a loose carrick bend untying, so that it is prudent to seize ends to standing parts, especially if the knot is to be left in place for a long time or if safety is an important factor, as in towlines, anchor

rodes, or a spring line.

The carrick bend is easily mistied, and the result is as unusable as the aforementioned granny knot. A proper carrick bend has one end up and the other down, and the same for standing parts. If both ends are up and both standing parts down, or vice versa, it is not a carrick bend and it will not hold. Many people have trouble with this geometry and do not practice enough to get over the problem. As a result, the carrick bend is not used as often as it should be — most of the carrick bends I have seen in use are my own. It is worth noting again that the reef knot (square knot) should never be used to bend ropes together, because it either capsizes and unties itself or it jams. Use a sheet bend or a carrick bend.

1

3

1. To start the carrick bend, make a loop in one rope and hold the other rope over it, as shown.

2. Bring the end of the second rope under the standing part of the loop.

3. Then bring it over its end.

4

5

6

CARRICK BEND

4. Now thread the end of the second rope up through the loop.

5. Bring it over its standing part and back down through the loop. At this stage, the carrick bend looks handsome.

6. But, when tightened, the prince turns into a toad.

Ashley's Constrictor Knot

This very useful knot, another invention of the remarkable Clifford Ashley, is not particularly well known. It has been promoted in Hervey Garrett Smith's books, but still, very few mariners are familiar with it. The constrictor is a simple knot — a variant of the plain whipping, only with fewer turns. Its great advantage is that it can be tightened efficiently, and once tied, any slack taken up never escapes as it does with a reef or other knot. (There is nothing more futile than trying to draw a reef knot up very tight, holding it with a finger, and having much of the strain disappear as the second overhand is taken up.) With Ashley's constrictor, tremendous strain can be developed in the rope by pulling between feet and both hands — the feet can hold a bowline and the hand end can be tied to a winch handle or other suitable rigid object — and all the tension applied stays in the knot.

Ashley's constrictor is the ideal knot for binding tightly, as in making temporary repairs to a cracked wooden spar or tiller. It can be used as a substitute for hose clamps in many applications, and it can probably constrict beyond the point at which most hose clamps start jumping threads. Seizings applied with a large mallet or steel bands applied with a heavy banding tool are probably more powerful, but the former procedure is time consuming, and tools for the latter are usually not available. Reef knots should be used wherever heavy constriction is not required, as in furling sails and tying anchors down, because they are easily untied. Once tight, Ashley's constrictor must be cut off.

On a modern yacht the best applications for this knot are in repairing cracked tillers and in tying to standing rigging. The standard laminated tiller is very fragile; it tends to crack without falling apart, becoming too flexible for its purpose. It only takes a few minutes to effect temporary repairs by throwing on a few constrictors. On EEYORE, the result was so satisfactory that no other repair was ever made. Cover the constrictors with Turk's heads and varnish over the whole thing, and it is more attractive, and probably stronger, than a new tiller.

While thinking about repairing broken tillers, it occurred to me that these constrictor knots could be drawn up very tight by pulling them between opposite cockpit winches. Do not use nylon or small line and do not overdo it — serious injury could result if the line is stressed to the breaking point.

It is very hard to tie anything to stainless steel rigging. Some knots, such as clove hitches, untie themselves and most of the rest slide down. A quick and secure way to make a tie stay put on a shroud is to wrap the cable with tape and then, over the tape, tie a constrictor, doubled, taken up with a pair of pliers. Plan to leave it on the stay. Seizing is much more time consuming to apply and does not work any better.

 **CHAPTER 1**

ASHLEY'S CONSTRICTOR KNOT

1. Tying Ashley's constrictor knot involves putting a turn on top of a simple overhand knot, so you have to go around twice.

2. Here the overhand knot is being tied with the two ends, under the extra turn.

3. One end emerges from each side of the turn and the knot is pulled tight.

1

2

3

1

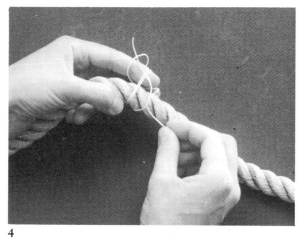

4

DOUBLE ASHLEY'S CONSTRICTOR KNOT

1. The double Ashley's constrictor knot is tied with two turns. You start by making three wraps around. Holding the wraps on a finger, as shown, keeps them orderly and makes tying the overhand knot easy.

2. Bring one end under all of the wraps.

3. Bring the other under to tie the overhand knot.

4. An extra turn on the overhand can be held by two wraps, making this constrictor even more secure. Pull it tight by its ends. Before final tightening, this knot can be capsized and untied by pulling on one of the ends, but once it is pulled very tight and with its ends trimmed close, it can only be cut off.

2

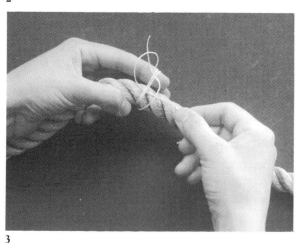

3

Bowline on a Bight

We come now to a pair of classic knots which appear in virtually all knot manuals. The usefulness of these knots is less clear-cut than for the preceding group.

I had a bit of trouble learning the bowline on a bight as a Boy Scout and I long thought the effort had been in vain. I am amused by the contrived applications of this knot which appear in many knot books: hoisting unconscious people, slinging ladders, hanging blocks with hooks so that there is a double bearing surface, and so forth. But the knot is fun to learn and occasionally useful for putting a nonslipping loop or two in the middle of a rope.

I am pleased to be able to report that I recently had occasion to use a bowline on a bight in a situation where no other knot would have been satisfactory. I was relaxing in IPHISA's cockpit at the old public dock in Roadtown, Tortola, when a power boat ineptly entered the neighboring berth. We were only separated by a piling and I had to

do some hard pushing to keep her stern away from our topsides. The other skipper was unfamiliar with the principle of spring lines, so I had him push while I tied up his boat. It turned out that he did not have a line on board which could be used for a spring, and that there were only three short lines suitable for bow and stern, which were already rigged. The anchor rode, of very light nylon, was all that remained to use for a spring and bow line; one of its ends was eye spliced onto a thimble which was attached to the anchor by a frozen shackle, and the other end disappeared through a deck pipe. I tied a bowline on a bight which I got over a piling with a boat hook, so that I was able to lead one part of the anchor line to the bow, and the other to the stern as a spring line.

Another application of the bowline on a bight is referred to in the above text relating to the sheet bend. All in all, it will not be called for very frequently, but when you need it, you need it.

1

2 3

3 2

4

1. The bowline on a bight is made by passing the bight through an overhand loop.

2. Then pass the loop and standing part through the bight.

3. This produces the familiar bowline geometry.

4. Here is the finished knot, which can be put over a piling to provide two dock lines.

Sheepshank

When standing rigging was made of rope, and topmasts and bowsprits were shipped, the sheepshank knot was quite useful for taking up slack. Although it is now excluded from many knot books, many yachtsmen will eventually have the need to shorten a rope without adjusting its ends. The sheepshank is the only knot for this purpose.

78. The LINEMAN'S RIDER or LINEMAN'S LOOP KNOT is the best of several loop knots that are tied in the bight and that are suitable for hauling in a direction parallel to the axis of the rope.

First Method

Fig. 78A: Twist a loop in the bight one full twist. Fold this loop up.

Fig. 78B: Pull A down through the center.

Fig. 78C: The completed knot.

Second Method

Fig. 78D: Form a loop in the bight.

Fig. 78E: Form another loop at point A in the first loop.

Fig. 78F: Pass A over the top and down through B on the other side. Burger (1914-1915), who first published this excellent knot. writes as follows: "Linemen and especially telephone men often use a knot which they term the lineman's rider. It is absolutely secure and will hold from any point upon which it may be drawn." Drew (1931) likens it to the bowline "in that it will not jam." "It is often used," he says, "when a crew of men are to pull on a rope and it is convenient for each man to have a loop rather than pull on the straight rope." Wright and Magowan (1928) call it the *butterfly noose* and recommend it as a middle loop for mountain climbers, a purpose to which it is perfectly adapted.

from Cyrus Lawrence Day
The Art of Knotting and Splicing

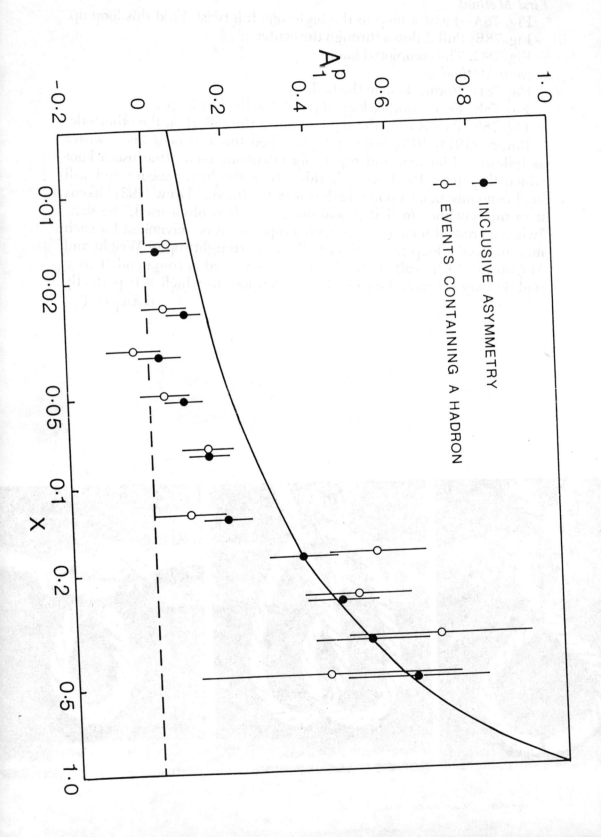

1

2

3

4

1. To shorten a rope with a sheepshank, first form the slack into parallel loops.

2. Make a half hitch in one of the standing parts. Slip it over the adjacent loop.

3. Repeat the procedure for the opposite end.

4. The finished knot. It will not capsize under load and can be easily adjusted by pulling more of the loops through the hitches.

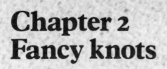

Chapter 2
Fancy knots

Before radio and widespread literacy, sailors needed a hobby. Some whalers did scrimshaw, but for most, fancy ropework was the answer. Hundreds of man-years went into the development of an oral tradition encompassing several hundred knots. The main hobbyist activity today is square-knotting (now called macramé). The number of present-day yachtsmen seriously interested in fancy knotting as a hobby is small (and I am not among their number). Yet it is unfortunate that so-called fancy ropework has fallen into such total disuse among yachtsmen; it still has significance as an aspect of practical seamanship. These knots are not purely decorative — they can and do serve many basic practical purposes. I derive personal pleasure from tying a star knot, and I am dismayed by sailors who do not even know how to wall-and-crown or to short-splice. The resurrection of a dead tradition is not at issue. Knowing and using a few of these knots indicates that a sailor pays some attention to detail and is interested in doing things right.

The only application of fancy knotting that is still standard today is the Turk's head on the center spoke of the helmsman's wheel. Another on the boat hook would be an improvement, and many other hand- and footholds would also benefit from this treatment. Every yacht which regularly visits strange ports should have a heaving line, especially if she does not have an engine (sooner or later, every yacht does not have an engine!). Finally, inasmuch as the ship's bell is an anachronism required by the Coast Guard, the bell rope seems the appropriate place for a star knot.

I do not give complete instructions for making a proper bell rope or signal-cannon lanyard. Several of the books listed under references do. I prefer to combine the diverse techniques into an original creation (which is how the old boys did it) rather than copy a pattern. While tying the six-strand star knot for the accompanying photographs — no one will ever succeed in making this knot perfectly clear — I visualized the perfect project incorporating this knot. I would use six strands of ¼-inch Dacron braid of three different colors (red, white and blue, for example). These would be whipped to a ¼-inch dowel and, after the star is completed, the strands would cover the dowel as coachwhipping. At the other end, a loop could be made in sennit and finished off with a standing Turk's head. This would make a much neater and more colorful bell rope than the traditional type with several additional knots. I plan to make jib halyard snap-shackle pulls from three-strand rope. They will be eye-spliced on and will end in manrope knots. I am opposed to decorating a yacht until it looks like a Victorian front parlor or a giant charm bracelet, but bell ropes and shackle pulls, among other such things, are functional and attractive.

Wall and Crown Knots

These are the simplest of the many multi-strand permanent knots which can be tied in a rope end either to prevent unravelling or to raise a knob, or both. Walls and crowns are not generally used as separate knots, but are combined into the wall-and-crown which also serves as the basis for other more complex knobs. The wall-and-crown is not really large enough to serve as an efficient stopper, but it is a most convenient quick solution to the common problem of what to do with an unwhipped rope end.

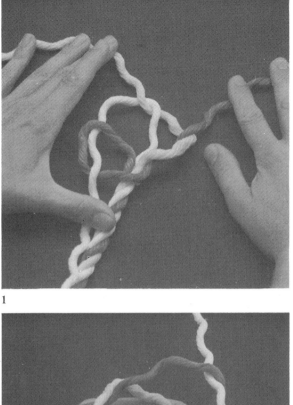

1

2

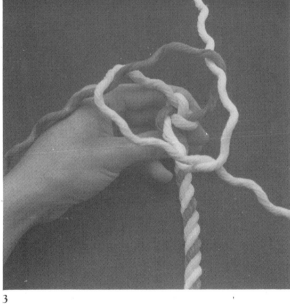

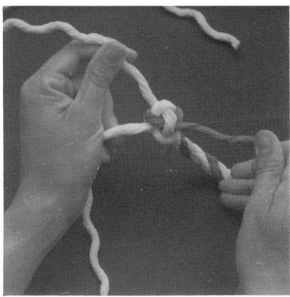

3

4

1. Making the wall knot. The knot should be made so that the strands continue the direction of the lay. Each strand comes up under its neighbor. If it is made in the other direction, it will not stop the unlaying of the rope, but run down the rope as it is tightened.

2. The wall knot drawn up.

3. Putting a crown knot on top of the wall knot. Each strand goes under and out from its neighbor, rather than up and under as in the wall.

4. The wall-and-crown knot drawn up.

Manrope Knot

A manrope knot in the end of a bucket rope.

This easily tied knob has several advantages over the wall-and-crown knot from which it is derived. To make a manrope knot, simply tie a wall-and-crown with longish strands and then lead the strands through the knot again. In other words, the manrope is merely a doubled wall-and-crown knot. Properly drawn up, the manrope knot will not loosen and untie itself. The strand ends, which point up the rope, can be backspliced into the standing part, making the knot even more secure and considerably neater.

This elegant and simple knot should be in every sailor's repertoire. There is no substitute for a good knob on the end of a bucket rope or a centerboard pendant, among other places, and the manrope is one that everybody can master.

Most ropes tend to unlay themselves and the strands come apart if handled. When tying multistrand knots such as the manrope, one must prevent this from happening. Ashley's constrictor knot can be used as a quick and handy whipping to limit unlaying of both rope and strands (though I prefer a hot knife for the latter).

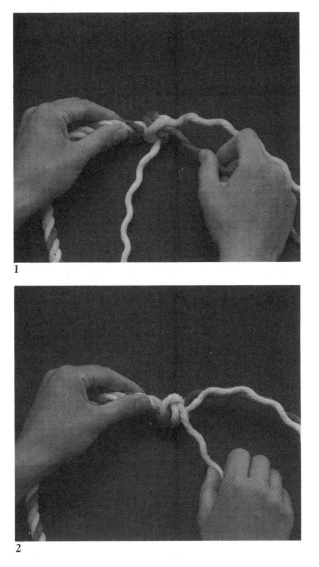

1

3

2

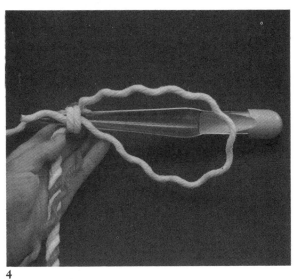

4

1. A manrope knot is a wall-and-crown with each strand led through the same path twice. Here a strand is being tucked back under one of the loops of the crown, after following itself all the way around the knot.

2. The same operation with another strand.

3. The crown is now double-stranded.

4. The knot is usually finished by tucking the strands down through the loops of the wall and backsplicing them into the standing part of the rope.

Matthew Walker Knot

Whoever Matthew Walker was (or whoever invented this knot), he deserves considerable credit. I am continually amazed that such a deceptively simple sequence of tying produces such a beautiful result. A Matthew Walker is more easily tied than a wall-and-crown, but few are familiar with it. I have trouble with this knot, apparently because the steps involved seem to be unrelated to the goal. In most knot tying, as in life in general, work usually consists of filling in the blanks provided by a mental image of the finished product. But in tying a Matthew Walker knot, one seems to be performing the arbitrary steps of a magic trick; consequently, I tend to forget how to do the trick. More practice is needed and, as the matter fascinates me, will be done.

A Matthew Walker knot is perfect for preventing a rope from passing through a hole slightly larger than its diameter. I have rigged a lanyard on CYCLURA to prevent clothes in the hanging locker from swinging; a Matthew Walker keeps the end in its hole in the bulkhead and is visible in the saloon. Where a figure eight would strike some people as crude or slovenly, the Matthew Walker attracts favorable attention. This is one of the best decorative knots and can be used in bell ropes, knife lanyards, and the like. There are many variants that can be found in the more compendious knot books.

As in all splicing and multistrand knots, attention to detail is critical. The Matthew Walker should be tied over a whipping or constrictor which holds the strands together. The knot must be carefully drawn up to cover this stopping; failure to do this can result in a tangle rather than a knot. After the knot is tight, the ends must be finished off.

1

2

3

4

5

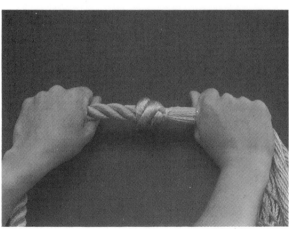

6

1. Beginning a Matthew Walker knot. The first step is to stop the strands — the Ashley's constrictor works well and is shown in place here. Next, take one strand and make an overhand knot around the standing part.

2. Another strand making its overhand within the first overhand. Note that the end comes through the first overhand before it goes around the standing part.

3. The same pattern is repeated with the third strand, which is shown emerging from the two previous overhands, before going around the standing part.

4. The third strand completes the third overhand knot. Matthew Walker knots can be tied with more than 20 strands; simply follow the same procedure with each strand.

5. Tightening a Matthew Walker knot. This knot requires careful working and tightening. If you just pull on the ends, you do not get a knot; just a tangle of ends. In tightening the knot, work it down over the whipping that was used to stop the strands.

6. A finished Matthew Walker knot tied in nylon rope. The strands have been stopped with a second Ashley's constrictor and will be trimmed with a hot knife. Another way to finish this knot is to crown the strands after the basic knot is tied, run the strand ends down through the knot, and whip or backsplice them to the standing part.

Rope Mats

The simplest and most decorative mat is a four-, five-, or six-bight Turk's head, flattened out. This makes a round mat with a hole in the center which can be fitted around a deck block or pipe to absorb the blows. Many of the traditional functions of such mats are now made obsolete by developments such as rubber-shell snatch blocks and spring-loaded deck blocks. By the same token, some new applications have appeared: such mats would serve well around certain types of spinnaker pole chocks, for example. The beauty of these mats is that they use up scrap material, are easily made, provide better protection than rubber or other alternatives, and do not have to be glued down.

The other application of mats is underfoot. A longer pattern is needed, and one of the old standards is shown here. There are many others which vary in the length-to-width ratio. Such mats are useful when a yacht is permanently at dock and dirt tends to get tracked aboard; insisting that everyone remove shoes is futile, especially with customs officers and other public servants. One mat on the dock and another on deck provides double protection. These mats can be cleaned easily by dragging overboard and, if made of nylon, function better wet. Some traditional yachts have such mats glued or tacked to the steps of companionway ladders and elsewhere.

The major work in making rope mats is not in weaving them, but in sewing the backs together. A hefty needle and sailmaker's palm are essential and the more stitches put in, the longer the mat will last.

SMALL ROPE MAT

1. Figuring out the geometry and laying out the knot is the hardest part. For simplicity of illustration, the four-bight Turk's head has been chosen. Each of the four loops interlocks with each of the others. Once the bights are properly arranged, to proceed, simply lead one of the ends on through the knot following the established path.

2. Three "leads" of the rope have been completed. More could be made. The finished mat is the result of considerable careful tightening and adjusting. Mats which will be walked on should be sewn together on their undersides.

1

2

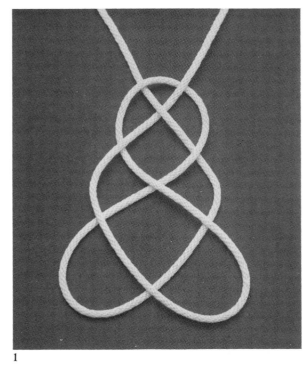

1

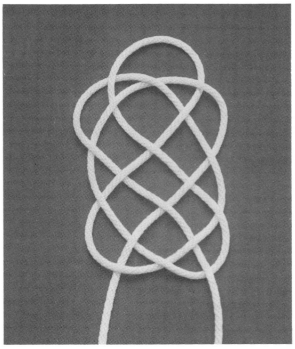

3

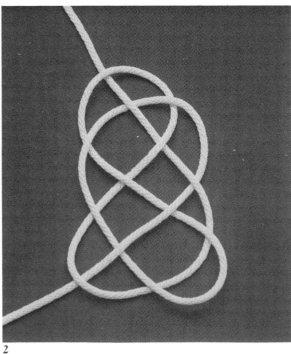

2

LARGE ROPE MAT

1. This eight-bight pattern is called the "ocean plat" by Ashley. To lay it out, start with a simple overhand knot. Pull out the two bights (leaving the ends running through the central loop). Give each of these bights a half twist and lay one on top of the other, as shown. The pattern has five bights at this stage.

2. One of the ends is now brought around and led under the first, over the second and third, and under the fourth strand it crosses.

3. The second end is led similarly around the other side, weaving alternately over and under the strands.

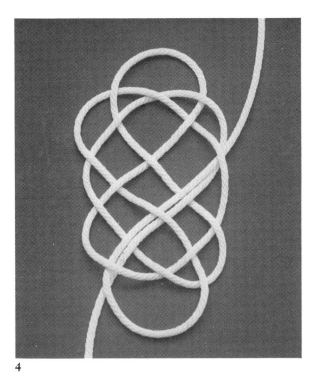

4. As the end is led back into the knot, the final (eighth) bight is formed. Two or three leads are usually sufficient to complete mats in this pattern.

5. Again, careful tightening and adjusting is necessary for a neat result. If the mat will be walked on or subjected to other hard use it must be sewed together at the back. The more stitches, the sturdier it will be.

4

5

Monkey's Fist

The monkey's fist is the most popular of all fancy knots, not because of its traditional application in heaving lines, but because it makes an attractive key fob. Small monkey's fists are made up commercially and sold for this purpose in nautical stores. Anyone can tie this knot, however, so there is no need to buy them. The advantage of doing your own is that you get the size you want and can adjust other details to your needs.

A monkey's fist can cover a round or cubic object. For heaving lines this knot can be lead or another heavy material, while a wooden core would make a key fob buoyant if it were dropped overboard. Some fiddling is required to find the right size of rope and number of turns to properly cover the inclusion. For the standard three-turn monkey's fist, the core can have a circumference up to about eight times the rope diameter, so that a ⅝-inch diameter ball can be covered with ¼-inch cord. The standard monkey's fist can be made with two to four turns successfully; with five or more turns, the knot will not hold its shape permanently. If one is intent on a project where more turns are needed, there are several other types of monkey's fists to be found in other sources

The monkey's fist geometry is simple and satisfying. It can be represented by three rings oriented in three planes perpendicular to one another. The first ring is inside the second, and the third is within the first, but outside the second. Each ring is within one ring and has the third within it. This structure cannot be disassembled without breaking the rings, and visualizing it in the abstract is a tremendous aid to tying the knot. The greatest difficulty in making a monkey's

A heaving line.

fist is in making the transitions between the rings neatly. If the initial route appears awkward, remove it and find a smoother transition path. As with most fancy knots (and many plain ones) careful tightening is essential. With this knot, tightening should take longer than tying.

Monkey's fists can be tied hollow — without an inclusion; this works best with two or three turns to each ring. Hiding the rope end, with a figure eight knot in the monkey's fist, works well. The best fob is made by burying both ends tied together, leaving a clean loop for the keys. This last alternative requires considerable additional effort, but the result is much neater than any other method.

1

1. To start the monkey's fist, hold the rope end at the back of your hand between your two middle fingers. Then wrap the rope around your fingers with two turns, as shown here. This forms the first circle.

2. The turns of the second circle are loosely made over the first at right angles. The end, tied in an overhand knot, can be seen; it is to remain buried within the completed monkey's fist. If some sort of solid core is used to weight the knot, both ends of the rope should lead out of the knot. One can be spliced into the other, either in a short splice, if the actual heaving line is to be of a different cordage, or in an eye splice, if the monkey's fist is being tied directly in the end of the heaving line.

3. The second turn of the second plane is placed below the first.

2

3

MONKEY'S FIST

4. The transition to the third circle is made by passing the end through the first set of turns just below the point where they lead into the second circle.

5. Bring the end up so it passes outside the second circle and inside the first. The third circle is thus inside the first, but external to the second.

6. Completing the first turn of the third circle and beginning the second.

7. Finishing the second turn of the third circle.

8. Tightening—This is one of the knots that must be very carefully tightened. It is easy to become confused in pulling the slack through the knot and lose track of which direction you are going. It is useful, therefore, to temporarily mark the strand closest to the captive end, so you always know where to start again should you get lost.

9. The completed monkey's fist.

4

5

6

7

8

9

Heaving Lines

A proper heaving line is the single piece of equipment which could be most easily added to the greatest number of yachts with the greatest possible benefit to seamanship. Tossing a coiled dock line works over a distance of a few yards, but there are many occasions when it is useful or essential to get a line across dozens of yards; this is when the heaving line saves the day. The monkey's fist is the best heaving-line knot. The general tendency is to throw at the person on shore, so while you may want to weight the knot somewhat by tying it around some kind of core, try to make sure that it falls considerably short of being a lethal weapon. The monkey's fist should have a tail about six inches long terminating in an eye splice. The line itself should be light and flexible braid, such as parachute cord. (A mistake made by some companies which market made-up heaving lines is to use polypropylene rope for both the line and monkey's fist. Polypro is much too heavy for this kind of a line and it lacks flexibility so that it keeps the shape of twists and bends and does not pay out smoothly.) The heaving line should be about 200 feet long and should be bent on to the monkey's fist at one end and to the rope to be led at the other end. It is thrown by holding the monkey's fist and a few loose coils and giving them a lateral swing. The rest of the line, which is held neatly coiled in the other hand, is free to follow.

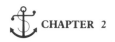

Running and Standing Turk's Head

These two knots are quite distinct in spite of their similar appearance and name. The running Turk's head is tied with a single strand and is free to slide if put on a cylindrical structure. The standing Turk's head is tied with multiple strands, usually three, and is anchored to its base. The latter is usually tied on stranded rope where the strand ends form a short splice, or cords passed between the strands are worked into a knot. It is a fancy way of finishing off an eye splice, such as on the upper end of a bell rope.

The running Turk's head is tied around a solid base, such as a dinghy oar, pushpit, boat hook, or more recently, a feminine ankle. If sufficiently tightened, this knot does not run, but forms a grip or a stop on a smooth pole, as in preventing the separation of oars and circular locks. The running Turk's head is easily tied and modified for various purposes by adding more turns. Variations on the Turk's head are catalogued in other knot books.

Turk's heads are useful to cover imperfections. They are commonly used at the ends of coach-whipping for this purpose, and anything else unsightly, such as an amateurish weld or useless screw holes, can be similarly covered. If a Turk's head or any other decorative knot is to be handled or exposed to the elements, it is wise to paint it. Use an enamel paint such as would be used for topsides, and thin out the first coat so that it penetrates the rope. White is traditional for most purposes except for standing rigging, where black is used. The Turk's heads on my dinghy oars are a year-and-a-half old and in reasonable condition even though not painted; I used nylon solid braid, which seems to shed most dirt.

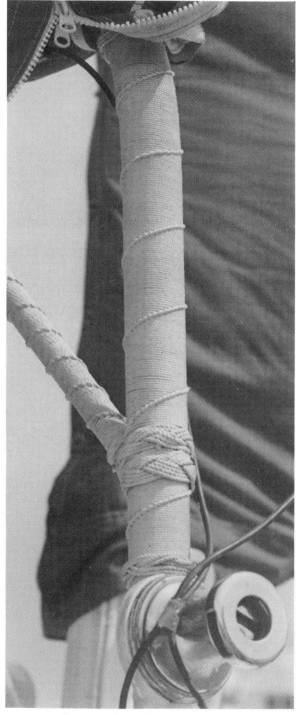

Running Turk's heads on a dinghy davit.

1

2

3

RUNNING TURK'S HEAD

1. Tying a running Turk's head. The first step is to wrap the rope around twice, and to pass one end over the other and then under a loop, as shown.

2. The two loops are crossed and the end on that side is woven between them. This operation can be repeated to make more complex Turk's heads.

3. When sufficient weaving has been done to cover the circumference, the two ends are brought together, starting the doubling of strands.

4

5

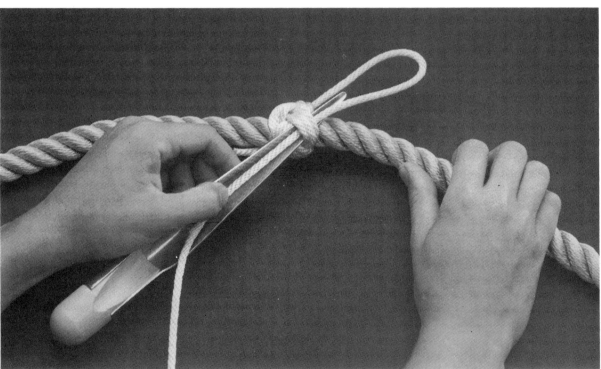

6

RUNNING TURK'S HEAD

4. Strands are doubled by following the weave with either end. When the strand ends meet again, the Turk's head is doubled.

5. A doubled Turk's head complete.

6. A doubled Turk's head can be tripled by leading the strands around again. A fid will be very useful for tucking the strands at this stage. The knot can be drawn up very tightly with pliers, in which case it will not "run," but stay put. The ends should be trimmed neatly where they emerge.

56

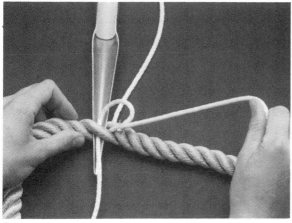

1

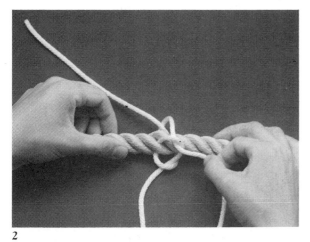

2

3

STANDING TURK'S HEAD

1. The standing Turk's head is done with a three-part cord made by seizing a short piece to the middle of a longer piece. This is then buried in the rope so that one end emerges between each pair of strands.

2. The three strands are crowned (by tying a crown knot) around the rope.

3. Another crown is made, with the ends pointing back towards the first crown.

4

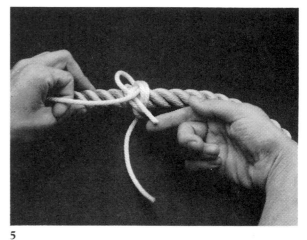

5

6

STANDING TURK'S HEAD

4. The upper crown is now doubled, by running each strand through one of its loops.

5. Here is the first indication that the right course has been set.

6. The second crown is now doubled, completing the knot. This Turk's head should be drawn up very tight, preferably with pliers; the ends should be trimmed close and pushed down into the knot.

Star Knot

Among the many hundreds of knots which form knobs on rope ends, the star reigns supreme in size, beauty, and sheer complexity. Anyone who can confidently tie a five- or six-part star from memory should be the life of many parties, if he can do it rapidly enough to hold people's attention. I have only tied a few and it takes me at least half an hour to get everything in its proper place, and longer than that to draw it up; if I am distracted during the first process, the project is apt to become an unsolvable maze. I do not believe that any combination of directions or illustrations can make this knot easy to tie.

Star knots can be tied with three to six strands. I have not tried more, nor have I seen examples published. The five-part star is used in the U.S. Navy on bell ropes. A three-part star knot on the end of a short piece of ¾-inch rope makes a powerful billy club and, as a knob to grab onto or to jam in a hole, the star has no equal due to its large size. I cannot imagine anyone spending the time to tie a star knot to keep a rope from passing through a hole, however — it is clear that the main reason for tying this knot is the challenge. It must have represented an awesome accomplishment for an illiterate sailor two centuries ago, when such knowledge was passed on orally — bartered, sold, or bestowed as a special favor. The inventor must have been both very clever and patient.

STAR KNOT

1. Throughout the tying of this knot, each step will be repeated in exactly the same way for each of the strands (you may use three to six strands). Begin by seizing your strands together, leaving the ends about a foot long. There are five distinct steps to tying this knot. Begin tying by making an underhand loop in each strand. The end of each strand should pass through the loop adjacent in the counterclockwise direction.

2. Step 1 completed for all the strands.

3. In the next step, each strand is bent back (clockwise) toward its first loop, and passes under the bight formed by the adjacent-clockwise strand doing the same thing; this forms a clockwise crown knot of all the strands.

4. The next is the trickiest step. Each strand is now led counterclockwise around its own loop, under its own standing part, past the loop adjacent counterclockwise, and down through the second loop away still going counterclockwise (see arrow). When each strand has completed this step, each end will pass through a loop that has been doubled. What we now have showing on the top of the knot is each strand going clockwise from one loop to the next, reversing course, passing under itself, and going counterclockwise to the second loop away.

5. The knot is now carefully drawn up to moderate tightness. The basic knot is tied—a star pattern in doubled strands has been created, and the remaining steps simply triple this pattern.

6. (Looking at the knot from underneath.) Lead each end so that it begins parallel to the other strand passing through its loop (see arrow) and then passes up through the center of the knot alongside the stem.

7. The final strand completes step 4. All the strands now emerge through the center of the top of the knot.

8. In the final step, each strand follows one of the pairs of star strands back across the top of the knot and is tucked down through its loop. For proper finishing, the strands should pass through all the intervening loops, emerging at the underside of the knot next to the stem. A fid is useful in completing the final step.

9. The completed star knot. Following careful tightening, the strand ends can be seized or backspliced into the stem.

1

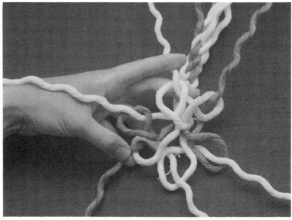

2

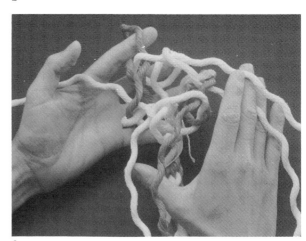

3

4

5

6

7

8

9

**Chapter 3
Splicing**

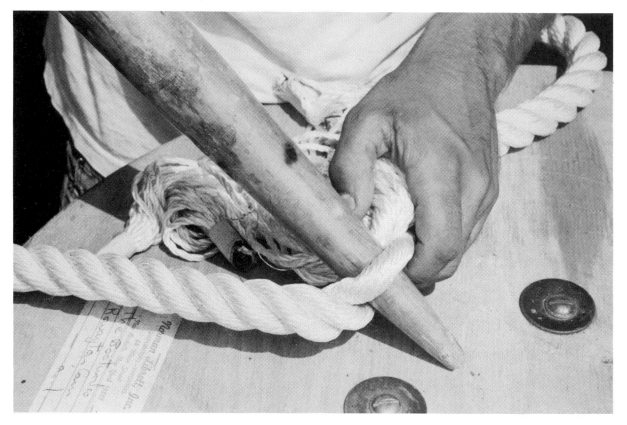

For some reason, there is a mystique about splicing that discourages many sailors from mastering this simple yet essential art. This is unfortunate, because the benefits of the splice — a woven, semipermanent union that is far stronger and less bulky than a knot — are many, and the problems are not formidable. Splicing three-strand rope is only a little more complicated than tying your shoe. Once grasped, it is straightforward and for the most part repetitive — the kind of pleasant work that mixes well with conversation and a cool drink in the cockpit after a sail.

Several different techniques are used in the splicing of different kinds of cordage. The splices in three-strand twisted rope that we will be concerned with use the technique of interweaving the strands of the rope parts being joined. Doubled four-strand sennit rope is spliced in a manner analogous to the three-strand interweaving method. Wire cable is sometimes spliced by exactly the same method as three-strand rope (although I neither use nor recommend this splice), but is much more easily and securely spliced by a technique of unlaying some of the strands and re-laying other strands in their places. Finally, splicing with yacht braid — which consists of a tube, the "core," within another tube, the "sheath" — involves extracting the core from the sheath and threading parts of each through the other. We will examine each of these techniques in detail as they apply to specific splices.

Eye Splice in Three-Strand Rope

Since modern yachting practice has rendered many splices obsolete, a sailor can operate quite effectively today knowing only a handful. If I had to select from that small group one splice that is a must, it would be the three-strand eye splice. The eye splice serves the same purpose as the bowline — to put a loop in the end of a rope — but is half again as strong. It is the most efficient and satisfac-

tory way to attach a rope end to a shackle or to make up a dock line (*all* dock lines should have eye splices in their ends).

The first step in making any three-strand splice is to unlay the strands of the rope end for a comfortable working distance, usually a minimum of 12 rope-diameters. A whipping should be applied at the proper distance from the end to prevent further unlaying.

Once the rope is unlaid, the end is bent around to the standing part to make the loop, and the strands of the end are interwoven with those of the standing part. Beginners often have great difficulty in figuring out how to get the splice started; indeed, even veterans who have made hundreds of splices sometimes get started incorrectly. Most splicing manuals solve this problem by carefully labeling the ends and strands in their diagrams (I have done this, in a sense, by using three-colored rope). Ropes seldom come coded in this fashion, however, so I think it is ultimately necessary to analyze the problem in such a way that a clear understanding results and the sailor is freed from dependence on books or pictures. The following is my attempt to accomplish this feat.

As with many problems, being able to visualize the finished product accurately is a giant step towards a solution. What we are trying to do here is to superimpose one three-strand rope over another, their directions of twist being opposite. If we were joining them end-to-end, there would be no problem, but joining an end to a middle requires a geometric compromise; the strands of the end must essentially "wrap" around the standing part. We begin by tucking two adjacent end strands under two adjacent strands of the standing part, the former crossing under the latter at right angles. If we try to tuck the third strand in the same manner, we will have turned our rope into a flat structure. In order to retain the roundness of the rope as nearly as possible, the third strand will have to reach back in the opposite direction to find its strand in the standing part. Since it will now be going in the same twist direction, it will have to reach around *over* its strand before crossing *under*, whereupon it will be oriented

properly with the other two end strands.

The splice is completed by continuing to weave the ends over one and under one in any order that is convenient, though each round of "tucks" should be completed before the next is begun.

Once it is correctly started, the critical element in a successful eye splice is proper strand tension — the three strands must be worked into the standing part so that the load is borne evenly. (This principle applies to all splices, but the problem is somewhat more difficult with the eye splice.) Unequal tension will result in the load on the line being carried by one or two strands rather than all three — in short, a splice that is probably weaker than a bowline. Proper tension is achieved by pulling each strand through each tuck with moderation; and by pulling on the loop with pressure almost sufficient to pull the strands out of their tucks after each round of tucks is made.

The tension of the yarns in each strand must also be uniform if the splice is to have maximum strength. This is especially a problem in nylon ropes of larger sizes, which tend to unlay themselves into separate yarns. There are two ways to deal with this problem, and a competent splicer should be familiar with both. The first is to keep each strand intact by whipping with two or three Ashley's constrictor knots, removing each as it begins to interfere with tucking. Carefully done, this results in an attractive-looking splice, but considerable patience is required to keep each yarn in its place and to retain the original twist of the strands. The other method is to let the strands fall apart into yarns, but keeping the bundles together. After each tuck, pull the yarns straight so that they lie even and parallel. This method results in a less attractive-looking splice, but

my experience has led me to believe that splices done carefully in this way may be stronger.

Four rounds of tucks are sufficient to hold the eye splice adequately in nylon or Dacron rope. Polypropylene, due to its slipperiness, requires six or seven rounds. Beyond these optimum numbers of tucks required to secure the interweaving of strands, further tucks add no strength. I recently counted 16 well-done tucks on a dinghy davit tackle. Intrigued, I investigated and discovered that the first round of tucks was poorly done and that, in effect, the whole splice was hanging by a single strand. In this case, concern with the trivial resulted in the critical being ignored.

There are several ways to finish off an eye splice. I simply cut the strands with a hot knife after the appropriate number of tucks has been made. Some purists, however, taper the strands by cutting out about a quarter of the yarns on the third tuck, a third of those remaining on the fourth, and half of the rest before making the last tuck. The cut ends are hidden by the rest of the strand, and the effect is attractive.

It is often said that a properly done eye splice is as strong as the rope it is made in. This is not quite true. When yachting ropes are tested with eye splices in each end, failure invariably occurs just in front of one of the splices. This means that when a rope is stressed to the failing point, it will break at a point of stress; the last round of tucks in a splice is such a point. In terms of normal usage, however, the weakness of the eye splice is negligible.

3-STRAND EYE SPLICE

1. To begin the eye splice, the rope is stopped with a clove hitch or constrictor knot 12 rope-diameters from the end, and the strands unlaid to the stopper knot.

2. The eye or loop is formed, and the fid is passed under a strand of the standing part opposite the stopper knot.

3. The uppermost strand at the stopper knot is tucked.

4. Fid is passed under the next strand away from the eye, and the strand end farthest from the eye is tucked.

5. The eye is turned over and the remaining strand end is tucked under the third strand of the standing part, after passing over it.

6. The three tucked strands are worked until they exit at roughly the same level on the standing part. The stopper can now be removed.

7. Select any strand, pass it over one strand and tuck it under the next strand of the standing part. Repeat with the second and third strands. You have completed one round of tucks. The succeeding rounds are done in the same way.

8. Finishing the third round of tucks. Notice that the rounds have been very carefully worked in. This is accomplished by twisting each strand until it lies fair and then by pulling alternately on the strands and on the eye. Nylon and Dacron eye splices hold with four tucks, while six or seven should be used with polypropylene.

9. The finished splice with the strand ends trimmed with a hot knife. They should be trimmed about one rope-diameter from the last tuck, or the last tuck will pull out under load.

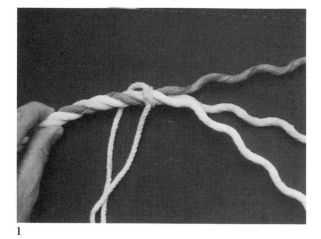

1

2

3

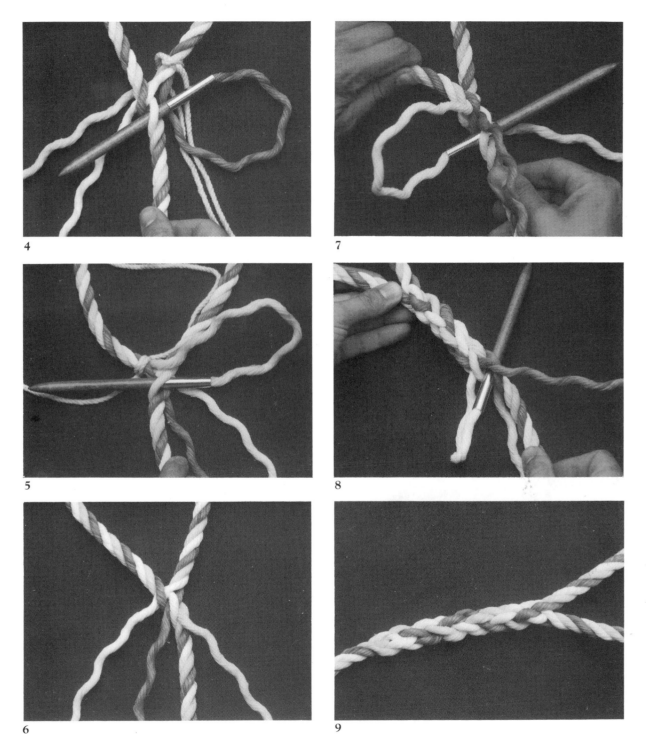

4

7

5

8

6

9

 CHAPTER 3

The Short Splice

The short splice is the strongest end-to-end
splice in three-strand rope. Carefully made, it
is comparable in strength to the eye splice. It
is used to lengthen dock lines, join hawsers
or ground tackles, to repair damaged lengths
of rope, and to make any circular or continuous rope that does not have to pass through a
block or sheave. It uses the same under-one,
over-one weaving technique employed in the
eye splice, but the geometric problem of
intermarrying the strands correctly does not
exist here. As all the ends are free, the rope
ends are simply joined with strands alternat-
ing — the orientations are all correct.

To begin, unlay the strands for a comfortable working distance, putting a temporary
whipping on each strand if necessary. Inter-
marry the strands of the two ropes, and secure them in the middle with a tight seizing.
As in the eye splice, the strands are interwoven, crossing over and under the strands of
the standing parts in the opposite direction
of twist (more or less at right angles). The
strands may be tucked in any order that is
convenient, but each round must be completed before the next is begun.

Three rounds of tucks on each side are
sufficient for ropes of nylon or Dacron; with
polypropylene, five tucks on each side are
required. When all the tucks are completed,
remove the center seizing and trim the strand
ends down to half an inch.

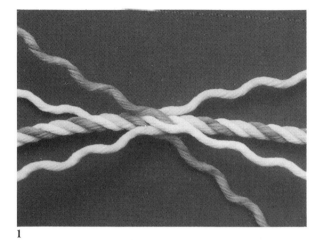

1

2

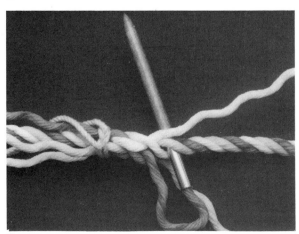

3

4

5

1. Starting the short splice. The two rope ends are unlaid and the strands are married so that those from one side alternate with those from the other.

2. Tie off the strands of one side to make easier the tucking of the strands of the other side. Strands may be tucked in any order that is convenient, but finish one round before beginning another.

3. Starting the second round of tucks, after the first has been drawn up evenly.

4. Five rounds of tucks have been made in one side.

5. Starting the first round of tucks in the other side. (Note: the rope has been reversed so work can be done in the most convenient direction.)

6. The tucking is finished with five rounds in each side. The ends should be trimmed with a hot knife.

6

Backsplice

The backsplice is the third commonly used three-strand rope splice. It is made by turning the strand ends back on the rope and interweaving them with the strands of the standing part. To prevent the rope's unlaying while the splice is being made, it is usually begun by crowning the strands in the direction of the lay. It then proceeds in exactly the same manner as the short splice — strand ends are led over and under the strands of the standing part.

Since it is not a load-bearing splice, the number of rounds of tucks is arbitrary and will depend on the intended usage.

The backsplice has three basic utilitarian functions: to serve as a permanent and very durable whipping, to thicken the rope ends as a permanent stopper, and to provide a handhold in a pull or pendant.

Besides the above uses, the backsplice is a neat and permanent way to finish off any of the ornamental or functional knob knots such as the manrope, Matthew Walker, or star knot in which the strands ends can be led back through the knot to the standing part. In this type of application, the strand ends can be tapered through the last few rounds of tucks in finishing off for a neater appearance.

1

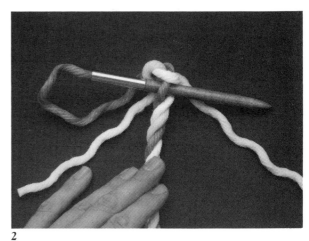

2

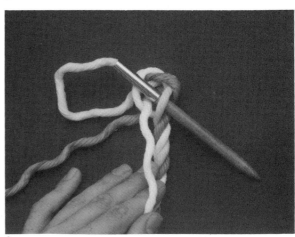

3

4

5

6

1. The backsplice starts with a crown knot. A whipping or stop knot is not needed except in ropes which unlay themselves easily.

2. In the first round of tucks, each strand passes under itself just under the crown knot.

3. The final tuck of the first round. Do not draw these tucks up tightly — subsequent rounds of tucks will take up the slack.

4. The second round of tucks. Proceed over one and under one, as in the eye and short splices.

5. All four rounds of tucks are in.

6. The finished backsplice with trimmed strand ends.

Yacht-Braid Splicing

A serious problem with splicing braid is that the finished product does not reveal its structure; as a result one has no model to work from. This makes it difficult to remember the somewhat confusing and seemingly paradoxical patterns of threading parts through other parts.

A wise precaution before beginning any braid splice is to tie a firm slip knot in the rope, several feet back from the splice, to keep the sheath and core in alignment while the splice is being made. To extract the core from the sheath, loosen and separate the sheath strands with a blunt instrument. Enlarge the hole, being careful not to damage the individual strands, until your

puller can be inserted under the core (see photo 1, p. 76). The loop of core is carefully pulled from the sheath until the end is free. The place where the core exits from the sheath is important in every braid splice; mark it clearly in ink. Threading the sheath into the core is accomplished by carefully working a tubular fid between the core strands and into its hollow interior. The sheath end is jammed into the fid end with a pusher, which is used to drive the fid and sheath through the hollow core. Exit from the core interior at the appropriate place by carefully working the point of the fid out between the strands again. This is the basic procedure for making all yacht-braid splices.

Eye Splice in Yacht Braid

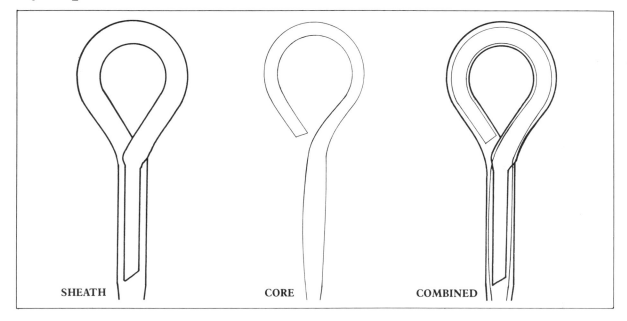

SHEATH   CORE   COMBINED

Again, yacht-braid splices can be very confusing. They are easy enough to make if one has an instruction book at hand, but who wants to have to rely on the printed page every time a splice is to be made? I have found it very helpful to visualize the paths of both the sheath and core separately in remembering how to perform this task. The sheath makes a loop and then pierces its own wall at the neck of the eye, tucking itself inside the core in the standing part. The core makes the same loop in the opposite direction (inside the sheath), but does not re-enter the base of the eye.

First, make a slip knot in the line about six feet from the end to keep sheath and core aligned. Measure off, from the end·of the line, the length of the loop plus the length of the fid you are using. Remove the core from the sheath at this point, being sure to mark it clearly where it exits from the sheath. Then pull additional core through the sheath —

about one and one-half fid-lengths. Starting at the mark, thread the sheath into the core for one full fid-length in the direction of the standing part. Then thread the core into the sheath, entering as near as possible to where the sheath was threaded into the core — this is the "crossover point." The core should exit from the sheath at the same point at which it was originally extracted. Now milk this core-sheath complex back into the sheath until the crossover point — the point where core and sheath switch positions — disappears into the sheath. Only the core end, sticking out through the hole in the neck of the eye, should be visible at this point. Trim it so it just sticks out of the sheath ⅛ inch or so. Tension the splice with a tackle or winch before trimming the core end. If trimmed off before the eye is loaded, it will later be pulled into the sheath, leaving a hollow section that looks unsightly but probably does not weaken the splice.

YACHT BRAID EYE SPLICE

1. Starting the double-braid eye splice. The core is extracted for a distance of one fid-length plus the size of the desired loop. This is done by pushing the sheath strands apart with the point of a fid, until the fid can be easily passed under the core, which is then pulled out. The final appearance of the eye depends largely on the care taken in separating the sheath strands. The core is now pulled out of the sheath for another fid-length beyond the point where it was extracted.

2. The sheath is threaded into the core for one-half fid-length, just ahead of where the core emerges from the rope. This and all other such threadings are done by inserting the fid between strands, rather than through them. The part to be run inside is inserted into the fid and a metal push rod is used to drive the fid and sheath or core through the hollow interior. The fid is brought out between strands as well.

3. The sheath, with fid and pusher, is just coming out of the core.

4. The core is now ready to be buried.

5. Insert the core into the sheath near the point where the sheath entered the core.

6. The core is threaded into the sheath for as far as the fid length will allow, whereupon the fid is drawn out of the sheath temporarily, and the core pulled through.

7. The core then reenters the sheath through the same hole, to make the rest of its journey around the loop.

8. The fid exits finally through the hole made when the core was extracted.

9. A tail will remain after the core is threaded through the entire loop. Cut this tail about one inch from its exit from the sheath. Work the splice back into the sheath by a combination of "milking" and poking with the pusher.

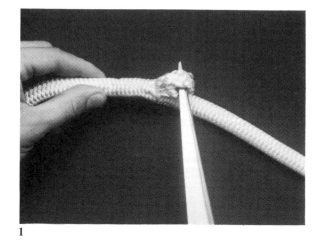

1

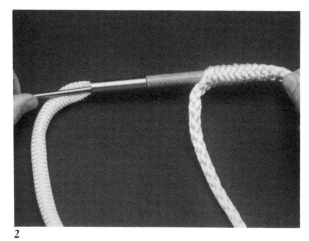

2

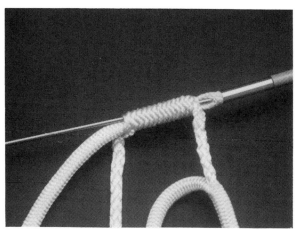

3

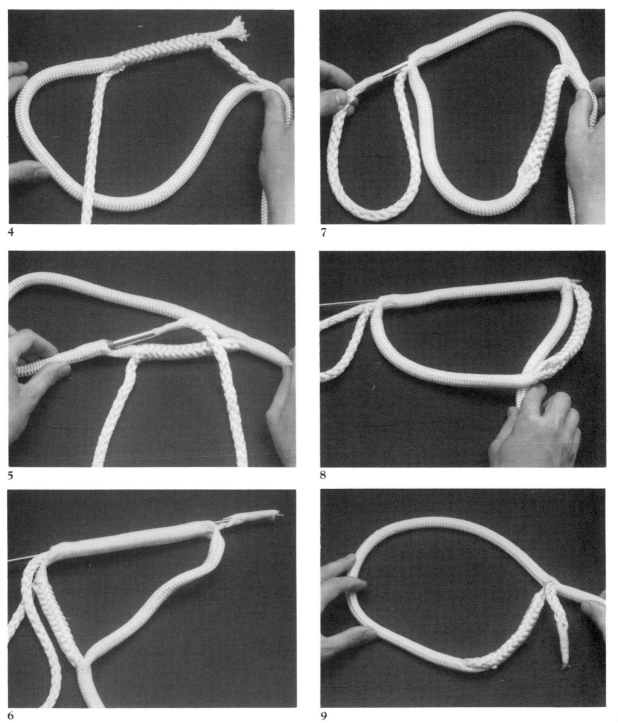

4

5

6

7

8

9

End-to-End Splice in Yacht Braid

This comparatively rare splice is the braided-rope equivalent of the short splice. The cores are extracted from the sheaths of both rope ends; the sheaths of each are threaded through the cores of the others and the stuffed cores worked back into the respective ropes.

Here is a brief rundown on the steps necessary to make the end-to-end splice in braid. Slip knots are tied in both ropes. The core of each is extracted one and one-half fid-lengths from the end and marked as usual. Each core is pulled out an additional one and one-half fid-lengths. Sheaths from the opposite ropes are threaded into the cores, entering one and one-half fid-lengths from the end, and exiting two and one-half fid-lengths from the end. The tails of the cores now cross over and run through the sheaths for one-half a fid-length, exiting at the same point where the cores were originally extracted. Tails are trimmed off flush at this point, and the cores are milked back into their respective sheaths. Some care is necessary in pulling and smoothing the whole splice into proper form and alignment.

Since this splice does not greatly thicken the rope, it is a good way to make a continuous line that has to run through a block or sheave.

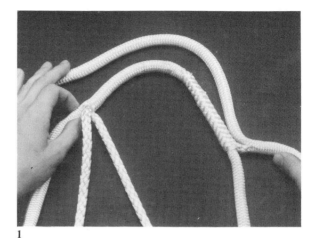

1

2

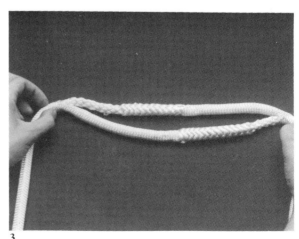

3

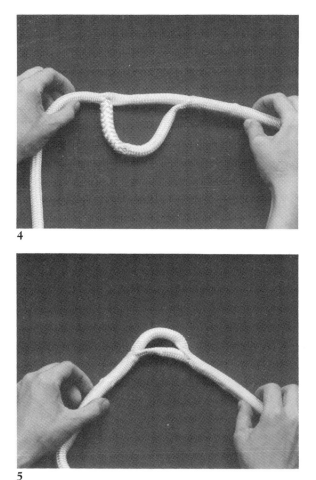

4

5

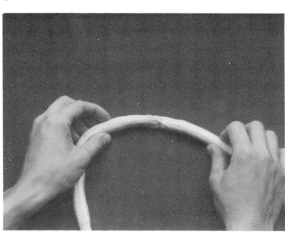

6

1. The double-braid end-to-end splice combines the same operations used in the double-braid eye splice, though the sequence and measurements are different. In this photograph, the core from the rope held in the right hand has been spliced to the hollow sheath of the rope held in the left hand. This was done by extracting the cores of both ropes one and one-half fid-lengths from their cut ends and then by pulling the cores out one and one-half fid-lengths more. The sheath is threaded inside the core for one fid-length, on the right, and the core is threaded within the sheath for the same length, on the left. The threaded core and sheath exit near the points where the cores were extracted from each rope.

2. The core-to-sheath splicing operation is repeated for the other core and sheath. The lower core and sheath tails have been trimmed here, while the upper ones still need cutting.

3. With both cores and sheaths trimmed, the splice is now ready to be closed up, by working the cores back into their sheaths.

4. Here, the upper core has disappeared into its sheath, and some of the portion which is sheath-covered remains to be worked in. The lower core and sheath are still exposed.

5. The splice is almost closed.

6. Completely closed, all that remains visible is the thickened rope and the splice where the two sheaths cross over.

Eye Splice in Doubled Four-Strand Square Sennit

This rope, which is beginning to become available in this country, is commonly known as eight-plait. Geometrically, it is the simplest of all the braided ropes and can be easily spliced in a manner quite similar to three-strand twisted rope.

Unlike twisted rope, in which all the strands follow the same helical path, in eight-plait, two of the strand pairs follow the "S" path and two the "Z," weaving under and over one another. When the strands of one part are woven into those of another, they are simply worked in on top of the strands with the corresponding orientation.

THE TWO HELICAL PATHS

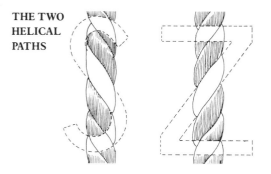

To make an eye splice in eight-plait, whip the line end a comfortable working length (at least 12 rope-diameters) and unplait the strands. (Note: until finishing off, the pairs will be treated as single strands — they never separate.) Determine the point of joining back to the standing part, which makes a loop of the desired size. Then, using a fid, weave the end strands in on top of the similarly oriented strands in the standing part. After four rounds of tucks, cut off one of each of the pairs and make two further rounds of tucks with the single strands. Finish the splice by trimming the single strand ends, leaving ½ inch or so.

1

2

3

4

5

6

7

1. The first step in splicing doubled four-strand sennit rope is to unlay the doubled strands. Do not separate the pairs. Next, form the loop to size. Tuck the first pair of end strands under a corresponding pair of the standing part. Make sure all end-strand pairs approach their corresponding standing-part pairs in the same coiling direction, rather than taking an abrupt turn into the opposite direction, which will weaken the splice. There is no particular trick to doing this, but if you do not pay attention to it, it will probably not come out right.

2. Making the first tuck with the second pair of strands.

3. With the third pair.

4. And the fourth.

5. The splice after four rounds of tucks.

6. Leave one strand of each pair behind and continue the tucking with single strands for another two rounds.

7. Trim off all strand ends with a hot knife, leaving a neatly tapered splice.

Rolled Eye Splice in 7x19 Wire Cable

Few yachtsmen know how easy it is to splice an eye into 7x19 wire cable. Most believe that wire splices require the experience of a professional rigger, and those familiar with this splice often distrust its simplicity, relying instead on the much more difficult and much weaker tucked splices.

To make the rolled eye splice, unlay three adjacent strands from the cable for a distance of the total circumference of the loop plus several inches, leaving the cable divided into a three-strand part and a four-strand part for that distance. Bend the four-strand part into a loop of the desired size and re-lay the three-strand part into the groove, working around the loop in the opposite direction.

This splice can be used temporarily if the ends of the two loops are seized to the standing part with several seizings of strong waxed-nylon line. For permanent use, the splice must be parceled and served with

wire. Align the two loop ends parallel with the standing part. Taper them by clipping the various strands at different lengths. Parcel with a single layer of black cloth electrical tape and serve with stainless steel serving wire. The serving should actually encompass a substantial portion of the loop itself (as much as two inches on an eye made from ¼-inch cable). This means that the loop should be made considerably bigger initially than it will end up. For eyes that will carry thimbles, make the eye about twice the size necessary to hold the thimble. Use a temporary seizing to hold the thimble, then close the eye snugly around it with the serving.

A properly served rolled eye is virtually as strong as the cable it is made in. I have eight rolled splices on CYCLURA — four halyard ends and four eyes on running backstay pennants. None of these has ever slipped or shown any other signs of weakness.

82

1

4

1. The cable is unlaid into two parts, one consisting of the core and three adjacent outer strands, the other consisting of the three remaining strands.

2. The loop is formed to size, and the parts are re-laid into the grooves.

3. Re-laying continues until the loop is fully formed.

4. When the cable parts reach the base of the eye, the ends are tapered by cutting the individual strands to different lengths. The strands are then laid parallel to the standing part and parceled and served.

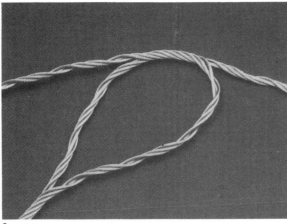

2

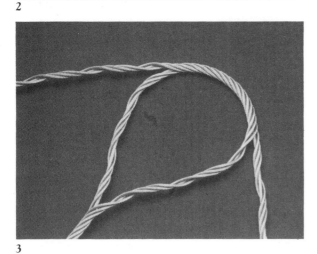

3

Tail Splice

Perhaps the most useful feature of yacht braid is the excellent splice it makes with 7x19 wire cable. With this splice, it is reasonably simple to securely attach an easy-to-handle rope tail to wire-cable halyards, rendering the dangerous reel halyard winch unnecessary.

For a successful tail splice, the rope must be twice the diameter of the wire cable. Having selected the proper size of rope, insert the cable end into a tubular fid and thread the cable into the interior of the rope for a distance of at least three feet. (The length is important here because the connection derives its strength more from the constriction of the rope on the cable than from the splice itself.) Now slide the sheath back from the core for a distance of 18 inches or so, and unravel about 12 inches of the core into separate strands. Divide the strands into three equal groups and use a Swedish fid to tuck them, short-splice style, under and over pairs of cable strands. Two rounds of tucks are adequate to secure the core to the cable — this will leave about 10 inches of strand ends to be cut off with a hot knife. Now pull the sheath back over the core and cable. Unlay five inches of sheath strands and divide them into three equal groups as above. Each of these groups of strands will be tucked under a pair of cable strands, but instead of continuing over and under, weaving fashion, you wrap the rope strands around their pairs of cable strands several times.

To achieve a smooth transition from cable to rope diameter, wax the sets of rope strands and taper the bundles after the first tuck.

1

2

3

4

5

6

1. Starting the double-braid-to-7x19-wire-cable tail splice. First, the sheath is pushed back and the core shortened by cutting off the last six inches. Then the wire cable is run into the hollow core for a distance of several feet. Since the splice derives most of its strength from the hollow rope constricting the cable, it is not wise to skimp on this. A tubular fid or tape over the cable end will facilitate this operation. Now the core is stopped with a constrictor knot six inches from the cut end, and the strands in front of the knot are unwoven.

2. The unwoven strands are divided into three equal groups. Each group of strands is tucked under two strands of the wire cable, using a Swedish fid.

3. Pull the strands under the wire cable strands tightly before removing the fid.

4. Two rounds of tucks are finished. The pattern is analogous to that used in the three-strand eye splice except that you go under two cable strands and over two, because 7x19 has six strands on its surface.

5. After a third round of tucks, the strands are hot-knife trimmed. If the cable end is within a few feet of the splice, pull the core tight over it and put a short seizing near it, which will prevent the cable end from sticking through the rope.

6. Now work the sheath over the core tucks and seize it to the wire six inches back from the cut end. Unweave the sheath strands to the seizing and divide them into three equal groups. Taper each group of strands by pulling them between a sharp knife and your thumb.

TAIL SPLICE

7. After tapering, wax the three strand-groups and work them into a point. This photograph shows the operation at three stages.

8. Tuck under two, as was done when splicing the core.

9. Instead of passing over two strands and then under the next two, a neater result is obtained if the strand groups are repeatedly tucked under the same two strands of the wire cable. Two rounds of tucks have been made here. After six or eight tucks, the strands are trimmed and the splice is finished.

7

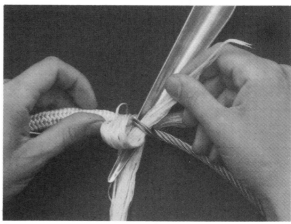

8

9

Splicing Tools

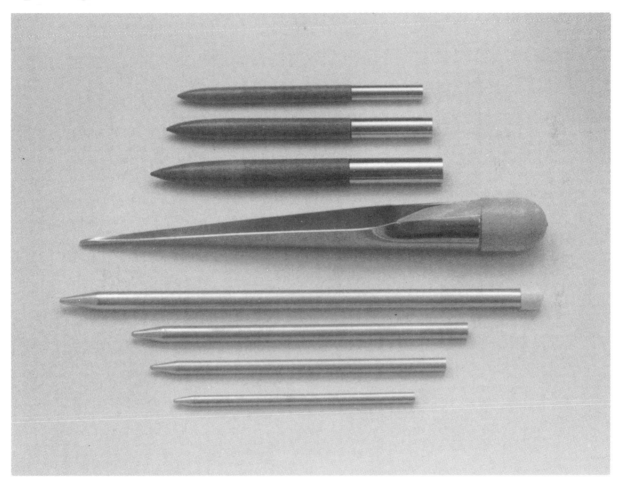

A dissertation could be written on fids, but a few designs are clearly superior to the rest. For most work on stranded ropes and for splicing 7x19 cable, the Swedish or hollow fid is ideal. With three-strand polypropylene, a short tubular fid works well because the hot-knife-cut strand ends are housed in the end of the fid and consequently can't catch in the filaments they are being tucked through. The smallest of my set of tubular fids is perfect for the weaving work involved in splicing doubled four-strand sennit rope.

Yacht braid requires a longer tubular fid and a pusher, which is no more than a stiff metal rod with a handle.

A pocket knife is needed to cut yacht braid (if this is done with a hot knife, the core can't be extracted). Use a hot knife for all other cutting of synthetic rope. No rope-splicing kit is complete without a roll of tape to prevent yacht-braid cores and sheaths from unraveling, and your ditty bag should include small stuff for whipping and stopping other ropes, as well as a needle and palm.

Chapter 4
Seizings, whippings, and anti-chafe

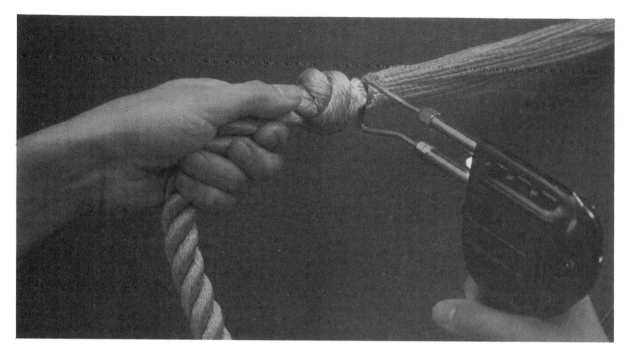

Improvements in the areas discussed in this chapter have been frequently ignored by the yachting public and press. I am constantly amazed by recently published books that recommend largely obsolete practices and dated materials like Manila and tarred hemp. I begin with a topic overlooked by most marlinspike authors, yet essential for the handling of modern ropes.

The Hot Knife

Nylon, polypropylene, and polyester rope should always be cut with a hot knife, preferably electric. (Burning knife-cut ends with a flame is a very inadequate substitute.) Perhaps the ultimate hot knife is an electric bench model that leaves both hands free to manipulate the rope; but a simple soldering iron fit with the appropriate blade will also do the job. The lightweight electric hot knives made for sailmakers are quite useful for detail work.

On a yacht, a hot knife is often needed when electric power is unavailable. I use an old knife heated over a portable propane torch. (Almost every kitchen has some old blade which can do service as a hot knife.) The knife should have a substantial mass of metal to hold heat and should have a well-insulated handle.

It takes practice to get a clean cut with a hot knife. The most common pitfalls are overheating the blade and overexertion while cutting. A hot knife operates by melting; if flames and charring occur, the knife is too hot. Since the knife does no actual cutting, minimal pressure is required. Most people, impatient when cutting large rope, start to push and saw and end up with an irregular cut. For a clean cut, first girdle the rope completely, saving the final separation in the middle for last. If a fixed electric knife is used, slowly rotate the rope with the fingers while resting it on the blade. With a flame-heated knife, attack a different part of the circumference after each heating. If this is not done, a poor cut will result.

For small and fancy work, a small hot knife comes in handy. If you don't have one, improvise. Narrow chisels work well for many jobs.

Whippings

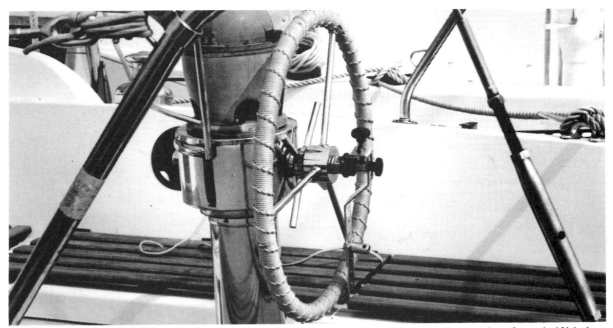

"French whipping": light line is wrapped around the wheel in a series of neat half hitches.

Whipping is almost always desirable to preserve a rope end, even if it has been cut with a hot knife. The best material for whipping is no longer marline or tarred hemp, but waxed nylon. The advantages of nylon are that it is very elastic, so that a whipping will not go slack even if one of the windings should loosen slightly; it can be sewn through the rope with a needle and palm; it is very strong, so that small sizes can be used; and it can be cut and fused with a hot knife.

The common or plain whipping that is shown in every marlinspike manual has little beyond its simplicity to recommend it. This whipping is not very durable; once any part of it snags, the whole is likely to unravel and fall off.

I prefer to lay on heavy whippings that are likely to last as long as the rope. To do

this, make several wraps around the rope and sew the ends of the small stuff through the rope, across the whipping, and back through the rope. This latter procedure is called "snaking" and should be done several times to protect the whipping from abuse. Heavy snaking on double-braid locks the core and sheath of the rope together (see photo sequence 1). On twisted ropes, snaking follows the grooves between strands (see photo sequence 2).

Whippings are not the only alternative for reinforcing a rope end. Don't overlook Ashley's constrictor knot, which is easier to tie, narrower, and as secure as any whipping. I use Ashley's constrictor under Matthew Walker knots, in wire-to-rope splices, and on strand ends. There are also fluids available that seal rope ends and "sleeves" that shrink when heated.

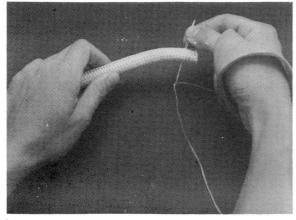

1a

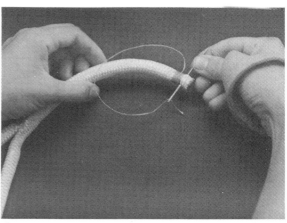

1b

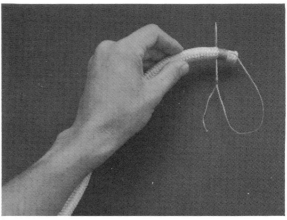

1c

WHIPPING

1a. The whipping line is first secured by sewing it through the rope. This can be done several times for added strength. The end of the line should be laid up under the main part of the whipping. The whipping itself consists of 15 to 20 tight wraps of the line around the rope working toward the end but stopping ¼ to ½ inch short of it.

1b, c. The whipping is secured and finished by snaking. This consists of sewing through the rope, wrapping the line across the whipping diagonally top to bottom (or vice versa), back and forth, until the whole whipping is securely bound.

1d. Secure the end of the whipping by sewing through the rope one final time and clipping it close.

2a. In twisted rope, snaked whipping is begun in exactly the same fashion: by sewing through the rope one or more times, the end laid toward the rope end, and 15 to 20 tight wraps of line made over the rope, working in the direction of the end.

2b. Snaking also proceeds in much the same manner, except that it is neat and convenient to sew through one rope strand at a time with the line emerging in the grooves between the strands.

2c. The finished whipping showing the diagonal snaking.

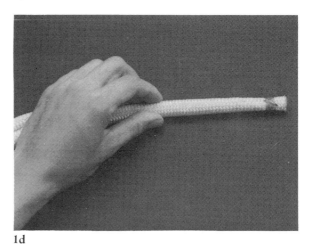

1d

2a

2b

2c

Seizing

Seizings, which are among the more versatile techniques available to a sailor, are used for attaching flag-halyard cleats, ratlines, for making terminal eyes in very large standing rigging, and for putting thimbles in hard nylon rope. They are structurally indistinguishable from whippings except that a seizing holds two ropes together, whereas a whipping only binds the strands of one rope. Moreover, an important distinction is that seizings must operate under stress.

Two ropes, or, more usually, the parts of one rope, can be strongly joined with a round seizing. First wrap the small stuff (again I prefer waxed-nylon thread, similar to dental floss) around the two ropes and lead the ends between the ropes, in front and in back of the wraps. Take a few turns around the wraps with the ends, then knot them. The round seizing is strong, but would work excessively should strain be applied to each rope.

The racking seizing is an improvement over the round seizing. Wrap the small stuff around one rope and then the other, figure-eight fashion. Apply considerable tension during this process and then cover both ropes with wraps and finish like a round seizing (see photo sequence, p. 94). My headsail sheets are made this way; and the sheets have sustained heavy winching without visible effect to the seizings.

Another useful application of seizing is for putting a sturdy eye in nylon rope that has become hardened due to immersion (such rope is almost impossible to splice). It may be necessary to do this frequently in coral areas where nylon anchor rodes chafe near the thimble. To make the eye, turn the rope around a thimble, lay it back on itself, and join the rope parts with two or three seizings.

1

2

3

RACKING SEIZING

1. Start the racking seizing by tying the thread end to one of the rope parts to be joined with an Ashley's constrictor knot; then weave thread between the rope parts in figure-eight fashion.

2. Turns should be laid down next to one another using considerable tension.

3. Cover the racking with a tight round seizing around both rope parts, and then wrap between them.

4. Finish the seizing off by tying the thread ends together. This seized loop will take heavy loads on either side independently without slipping.

4

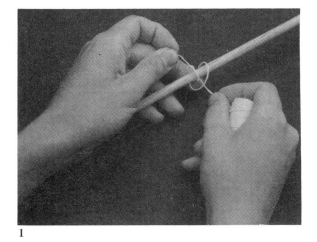

1

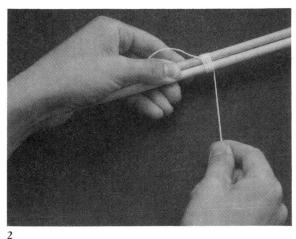

2

3

Lashings

Lashings are nothing more than heavy seizings used to join posts, spars, and other heavy pieces. The art of lashing consists of one basic trick: lay the pieces parallel to one another and put on several turns of solid-braid nylon. Thereafter, move the pieces to the desired angle and secure by making additional turns.

Lashing can be a useful technique in such situations as when a crack develops in a wooden spar. A splint can be lashed to the lame spar to strengthen it. To do this efficiently, use sizable timbers and a substantial rope, and tighten the lashings with the cockpit winches.

Serving

Whenever I find myself serving, which is mindless and time-consuming work, I recall the words of Hervey Garrett Smith: "Spending seventy-five dollars of one's time piddling around with a piece of string pays the kind of dividends not measurable in coin of the realm." Basically, serving is a covering with small stuff wound against the lay, for purposes of decoration, protection, or grip. For example, a stanchion covered with half hitching is served, as are footropes on bowsprits, to provide better grip for hands and feet.

The main use of serving on a modern yacht is to protect and cover spliced eyes in wire cable. Serving wire splices requires a different technique because the strength of the splice partially depends on the serving compressing it. First clip the protruding wire ends in the area of the splice for smoothness. Then parcel the splice by wrapping it with black fabric electrical tape wrapped in the same direction as the cable lay with minimal overlap. At this point, the serving is applied. Use stainless steel serving wire (made up of three to six individual wires) with the diameter about one-sixteenth that of the cable. Starting just above the tape, tuck the wire through the cable and lay the end towards the splice; this will be covered by the serving. Wrap the serving wire with considerable tension.

The ideal tool for this operation has yet to be invented although the classic serving board or mallet shown in the photographs works reasonably well. It is essential that the spool of wire be mounted on an axis parallel to the cable. If it is held on the mallet's handle, considerable extra twist is introduced. If the serving is laid down with inadequate tension, slippage along the cable is likely, causing gaps and eventually failure. If too much force is applied, the parceled tape will be squeezed out between turns, which is what happens anyway if several layers of parceling are applied or if plastic tape is used. Finally, excessive tension will break the serving wire. If the wire breaks, or if it is too short to finish the job, a new start should be made; there is no satisfactory way to finish two lengths midway.

To finish off the serving of a wire-cable splice, lay a few loose turns on and tuck the serving wire through the cable with a Swedish fid so it comes out between the second and third turns. Trim the end of the wire to about six inches and tie an overhand knot in it to make a good grip. Use pliers to pull on the knotted end while working the loose turns tight by hand. Finally, clip the end flush.

1. Parceling with tape.

2. Attaching the serving wire.

3. Laying down the serving with a serving mallet.

Anti-Chafe for Sails

Chafe can rapidly destroy sails. Ocean-going yachts usually sustain the worst chafe at the spreader tips. There are rubber boots made precisely for this purpose that can be seized on with waxed nylon thread. In a pinch, sheepskin or pieces of carpet can be sewn onto the tip. On small boats, rollers mounted on the shroud either above or below the spreader work well, but are not as neat and cost more than the boots.

After spreader tips, the biggest source of sail chafe is standing rigging. The chafe of aft lower shrouds and the running backstays on a boomed-out mainsail is substantial. Plastic (PVC) shroud covers, available for each size cable up to ⅜ inch, are the best solution. These are quickly installed and usually last about three years. Large genoas tend to chafe on the upper and forward lower shrouds during tacking. Either the traditional wooden rollers or lengths of PVC pipe mounted on the shrouds alleviate this problem. The wooden rollers are bulky and require varnishing. PVC pipes, installed before the terminals are fitted, can be quite small, with an inside diameter slightly larger than the cable; they are inexpensive and attractive.

Finally, chafing frequently occurs from deck hardware — especially lifelines and pulpits. On CYCLURA this is limited to chafe of the yankees on the bow pulpit when running or broad-reaching. Since the pulpit is already highly polished, the only additional solution is to sew a chafing patch on the portion of the sails affected.

Great harm can occur when hoisting a sail from the deck. Turnbuckles, especially their sharp cotter pins, can rip sails badly. Tape such snags or cover them with boots.

Anti-Chafe for Ropes

Due to the elasticity of nylon, unprotected dock and anchor lines suffer tremendous chafe. As a nylon line stretches and contracts, it saws back and forth on any point of contact. (Dacron running rigging suffers much less chafe because this back and forth motion is relatively small.) Avoiding abrupt changes in line direction is the most obvious anti-chafe measure. Unfortunately, many yachtsmen do not take advantage of this knowledge. For example, they rig their spring lines from the bow cleat forward to the chock, where it takes a sharp turn aft. Chafe at the chock is inevitable (and unnecessary since the line could be led aft from the cleat, over the rail).

But truing lines won't eliminate all chafe. Wherever the lines come into contact with anything they must be covered. Cloth is the classic covering but lately rubber sleeves have become popular. These sleeves fit over the rope and are made to overlap themselves. They are satisfactory but expensive. Plastic tubing works just as well and can be permanently installed on mooring pendants, anchor-chain spring lines, and dock lines. To work a line into a length of plastic hose, if the fit is tight, short-splice a small-diameter leader to the line and work the line carefully through the hose pulling on the leader.

Left: flexible plastic tubing is an inexpensive anti-chafe precaution for rope.

Facing page: plastic (PVC) shroud covers. Note the larger-diameter pipes on the lower part of the shrouds covering the turnbuckles.

Chapter 5
Line handling

In this chapter I will discuss various aspects of line handling and attempt to chart a course which avoids the major pitfalls. Because St. Thomas is one of the world's major yacht-charter centers, for 10 years I have had the opportunity to observe a very broad cross section of the possible errors in line handling (among other aspects of sailing). In some cases, these were a result of ignorance or simple foolishness, but there were also many instances in which logic had been brought to bear on the problem, albeit with some flaw. The latter situation frequently occurs when experienced sailors first deal with a new device or situation. Many other disasters in the yacht-charter business can be traced to small-boat practices being applied to large vessels where they don't work.

Novices are frequently unprepared for the developing load in a line. This can be observed frequently in dock tourists who derive some pleasure from catching a dock line. Several years ago, the replica schooner AMERICA was docking at the Charlotte Amalie waterfront and attracting quite a crowd. An able-looking fellow near me caught a dock line, but instead of taking a turn on the nearest cleat, he tried to pull this behemoth against the wind. Before he was dragged into the water, some more experienced sailors took the line away from him. Rule: never stand holding a line under load—put it on a cleat or take a turn around a post or bollard. (Note: since one often has to deal with volunteers in docking, even when help is a hindrance, the ploy of having eye splices on all dock-line ends works well. It is possible to give very clear instructions about their disposition.)

Handling Stressed Lines

If there is any likelihood that a line one is handling will come under a significant load, the line should be surged around a solid, immovable object. (The only exception that occurs to me is that of sheets on small sailing dinghies which must be hand-held to permit rapid response to changing conditions.) Tremendous calamities can occur in the handling of lines under load. The process of surging—taking a turn or two around a cleat, post, bollard, winch, or windlass drum—gives the sailor greatly added control over the loaded line through the agency of friction.

The worst accident to occur on a yacht of mine involved the laying of a mooring for EEYORE. My friend Larry Parker was at the bow ready to cast off chain from the Samson post. The chain was attached to a large truck engine, and when I gave the command to let her go, Larry's fingers got caught between the chain and the bow roller. He was badly cut, but, luckily, lost only blood.

One important lesson is that this accident was my fault. As captain I should have planned a safe way of accomplishing the task and above all, I should have carefully discussed the operation in advance, making sure that my helper knew exactly what to expect. In this instance, I rushed into the job assuming he could get along.

Casting off a line under load, as in this case, is always a tricky and potentially dangerous operation. The best way is to run it out over a Samson post or cleat until it is gone, keeping clear of the bitter end which can snap about wickedly when set free. Inexperienced sailors often make the mistake of trying to get the line or chain off the post and letting it run free. If a line is running out rapidly, as lines under load always are, it is easy to get tangled up in it. Some gruesome accidents result from this practice.

A properly placed cleat of appropriate size, or a suitable alternative, is absolutely essential on any boat bigger than a small dinghy which will ever be anchored or towed. It should be mounted on the centerline and permit one or two turns to run without jamming.

Many boats lack adequate cleats, bollards, or posts on which to surge anchor rodes and towlines from the bow. On boats longer than 30 feet overall, a windlass fills this and other functions well. (Windlasses are discussed elsewhere.)

When an anchor rode is being payed out, it should always be under tension, which is properly managed by surging a turn rather than holding it by hand. If the rode stops feeding smoothly through the deck pipe and you have it in your hand, it can be jerked out of your hand and really jam the hockle in the deck pipe. If, however, it is being surged on a bollard or cleat, there will be considerable length of line between the cleat and deck pipe so that the rode can be cleated down, and the hockle can be dealt with.

On many racy sloops, the bow cleats are located near the rail and are too small to accommodate the anchor rode without jamming, so that the rode has to be held when it should be surged.

To pull the rode in under tension, it must be removed from the cleat entirely, which may cause some scope to be let out; or worse, the tension may be too great to hold and a great deal will be let out before the rode can be belayed again. The latter operation is highly dangerous to fingers under these circumstances.

On larger boats, it is useful to have several stations from which lines can be surged and belayed. The full complement includes two bow cleats, an amidship cleat on each side, and a stern cleat on each quarter. On sailboats, several cleats are required on which sheets, halyards, and other running rigging can be belayed. Sometimes the docking cleats can be positioned to serve double duty in sailing.

Belaying

To "belay" is to make a rope fast to a cleat, bollard, Samson post, belaying pin or other solid piece. All belaying should start with a turn that can be surged. Any line that is belayed should be arranged so that it can also be surged from the same position.

Belaying on a bollard.

103

Cleating

The object in cleating is to make the rope fast *in a way which can be easily and safely undone*. To do this, pass the rope completely around the cleat, under both horns, before taking any hitches. Then cross over the top of the cleat, pass under a horn, and put a half hitch on the other horn so that the hitch and the cross-over lie flat along one another (see photo sequence 1). A rope belayed in this manner will not jam and will not uncleat itself. There is no purpose in piling on additional turns, crosses, and hitches, as these do not increase security but *do* make the undoing harder.

For cleats to function properly, they should, where possible, be mounted at an angle to the orientation of the lines that will be belayed on them. The first turn on a cleat should always be taken on the open side so that the rope does not press against the side of the cleat. If the cleat is oriented in the direction of the rope, subsequent turns of the rope may jam the first turn — sometimes there is no way to avoid such a situation. Taking the first turn on the closed side of a cleat can be disastrous because the subsequent turns will jam very hard if there is substantial tension.

Some books show rope crossing the cleat after the first turn and a half hitch on the horn towards the standing part of the rope, without ever making a complete circuit of the cleat. This is very poor practice, because only a short piece of the rope is in contact with the cleat and when it is under tension, the half hitch will tighten and be hard to remove.

I have encountered an almost unsolvable predicament with a dock line under load. The line in question had the appropriate eye splice, but it had been used to tie onto a deck cleat by passing the loop through the cleat's legs and around the horns. The end on the dock had been belayed on a cleat backwards. Belaying backwards means that the crossing turns are put on with the standing part of the line rather than with the free end, and, under load, the line cannot be removed. To get out of this predicament (which was probably perpetrated by a dock volunteer), another line had to be led to the dock and winched in to relieve the load on the first line to get it off the cleat. In some circumstances it might be necessary to cut the line.

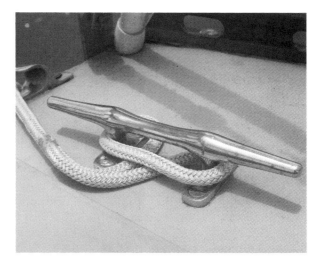

Above: an eye can be belayed on a hollow cleat by passing it between the legs and over both horns.

Facing Page
Above: a bow line with an eye can be belayed by passing it through the legs and over the aft horn.

Below: lines have to be belayed to solid cleats such as this in the conventional manner.

1a

1b

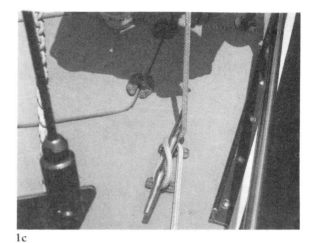

1c

1d

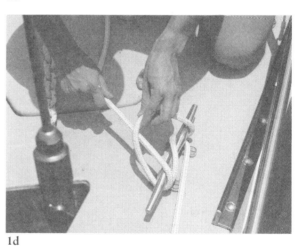

1e

1a. The first turn on a hollow cleat. Note the line leading to the open side of the cleat. This is the arrangement for light surging.

1b. The second turn on a cleat. Use this for heavy surging, when the loads are too heavy to hold with a single turn.

1c. The third turn crosses over the cleat.

1d. A half hitch is put on the horn away from you, so that the free part lies parallel to the third turn.

1e. The line belayed on the cleat.

Belaying to Other Structures

The belaying pin, now rather a rare phenomenon, is, in essence, a movable cleat. Lines are made fast to belaying pins in exactly the same manner that they are cleated.

Samson posts are sturdy wooden posts that serve as bow cleats. Their advantages over bow cleats are that they can be more strongly mounted, they are better suited to surging rope, and they can even handle chain. Several turns of chain will jam on a Samson post, but ropes must be belayed. Many sailors use a clove hitch for this purpose, but it is not suitable because it can jam so hard as to be impossible to untie. The tugman's hitch, in contrast, cannot jam and is easily cast off even under great load. Bollards, which differ from Samson posts in that they have a pin through them, are used in much the same way. Belaying on a bollard by putting half hitches on the pins works well enough, but the hitches can come off if the pins are small — again, I prefer the tugman's hitch. Boats with bowsprits traditionally have "bitts," which are like short Samson posts on either side of the base of the sprit. A rope can be belayed on bitts by going between them several times in a figure-eight pattern and finishing off with half hitches.

107

Handling Chain

Many yachtsmen have sworn off chain before they learned how to handle it. The tricks to chain handling are worth learning for the serious cruiser.

Any yacht which uses ground tackle a lot should have a chain rode and a windlass. Without a windlass, one is limited to relatively light anchors and nylon rodes, but in a blow, I want a heavy anchor and a chain rode. Without a windlass, this kind of ground tackle will not be recovered. CYCLURA's ground tackle is sorted out and reliable so that I can leave her untended while many

other yachts have an anchor watch.

Several books show clever devices that make chain handling without a windlass less arduous. Considerable ingenuity has been applied to the problems of getting along without a windlass and partial solutions have been found. Having skinned my hands and sprained my back pulling chain, I feel that a windlass is indispensable. I do not understand the apparently strong incentive to survive without one, because it is not a very expensive piece of equipment compared to the rest of the ground tackle. In any case, my discussion will proceed as if a windlass were the only means of handling chain worthy of consideration, which is, in fact, my opinion.

A windlass is absolutely required to handle chain anchor rodes on boats longer than 25 feet. Here the variable dimensions of chain links becomes a critical problem because the gypsy has to be well matched to the link size. I have tried to haul in chain with badly matched gypsies and it is almost impossible, as the chain either jumps out of the slots or jams and refuses to strip off the gypsy. On large yachts, a windlass or gypsy malfunction can be serious business, as I learned one dark rainy night near Los Roques, 50 miles north of the Venezuelan coast. Our anchor on a 50-foot sloop dragged and was now hanging down almost 200 feet in deep water. The windlass could not handle the load, so that lines had to be led to the cockpit winches by snatch blocks. Three strong sailors worked most of the night getting the anchor in. The only way to avoid this kind of hardship is to order gypsy and chain from the same firm at one time and to have a completely fail-safe system for getting the rode aboard.

Windlasses perform two separate functions well: hauling in chain, in which they provide mechanical advantage, and letting out chain, in which they provide adjustable friction. During both of these operations, there is a danger of getting toes and shoelaces caught in the works, so that care should be taken to keep the area clear of nonessential personnel, as well as of ropes, sails, and so forth.

On most windlasses, the handle is used to adjust the clutch to let chain out. Unless restrained, chain can attain considerable speed as it flies off the bow and, being massive, it has great momentum. If chain is payed out this way, instead of laying itself neatly out along the bottom, it will pile up in a heap which greatly increases the danger of fouling. For this reason, the clutch should never go completely slack, but should drag a bit as chain is going out. Once the anchor is on the bottom, my practice is to let the chain come up taut before letting out another few fathoms. For hauling in chain, the clutch is screwed in tight, and the handle is used to work a gear train. (In the case of power windlasses, a button is pushed instead.)

A function which most windlasses do not perform satisfactorily is holding the chain rode once it has been let out. The reasons for this are that windlass clutches tend to freeze if left tight, and the key-and-notch devices usually provided are not secure enough to be trustworthy. In addition, if chain under tension rides on a bow roller, a tremendous grinding noise results. The solution to these problems is to rig a spring line from the bow to the chain and to leave the chain slack. The windlass clutch should be left loose to prevent its freezing, but the key should be set in a notch. As a final fail-safe measure, the chain should be shackled to an eye in the chain locker or, better yet, be attached to something too large to pass the hawse pipe. On CYCLURA, I leave the spring line permanently shackled to an eye on the bow fitting; the other end carries a chain hook. The line is about 10 feet long and when sufficient chain is out, it is hooked on and additional chain payed out until the load is on the spring line.

As anchor spring lines are very subject to chafe, mine is completely covered in plastic tubing. If the boat sails around her rode, turns of chain will accumulate near the hook. To counter this especially severe chafe, use a short piece of chain between the hook and spring line.

Handling Idle Lines

Idle lines (lines not in immediate use) have a truly surprising capacity for creating havoc on shipboard. It is fairly clear that lines need to be ready to be put quickly to use. If they are not neatly stowed and arranged they can get in the way and end up in a tangle, creating delay and confusion in anchoring, docking, and numerous other operations. It is not so clear, however, that lines can be potential trouble even when they appear to be neatly dealt with. Many problems arise from ropes that are badly twisted, and twist is, for the most part, generated by the handling of idle ropes.

Most modern ropes can accumulate considerable twist without apparent ill effects. In any rope, however, twist will cause problems under some conditions — usually tension. (The problem is much more serious with twisted than with braided ropes, and the larger the rope diameter, the greater the problems caused by twist.)

To help clarify both the causes and the effects of twist, let us consider a familiar structure which is intolerant of twist — the garden hose. If a garden hose is coiled in a circle (actually a helix) on the ground and then extended by walking away with one end, numerous hockles (kinks) are produced — roughly one for each turn of the coil. The coiling introduces the twist, which is evident if the motion of the free end of the hose is observed as the coils are laid down: it rotates. As the other end of the hose is attached to a faucet and the twist does not travel down the hose very well, the twist produces hockles. If tension is applied, the hockles can break the hose. The solution here is to coil hoses in a figure-eight pattern, which does not introduce helical twist.

The circular (helical) coiling of rope produces the same effect, often causing needed lines to end up in a tangle. When a large coiled line is being payed out through a chock or block, for example, the twist tends to be confined between the block and the hands and accumulates there, eventually producing a hockle that will jam in the block.

I also suspect that twisting is the cause of much anchor dragging. My surmise is that considerable twist is put into the rode when it is coiled down; then, under considerable tension, this twist delivers a torque sufficient to break out the anchor. In both cases, the twist is being introduced by the coiling operation that presumably was intended to put things in order.

The solution is to avoid circular coiling in situations where it will lead to trouble. My rule is to coil rope only as long as the entire operation can be hand-held. I can coil 100 feet of ½-inch line without great difficulty; this seems a reasonable limit. Longer ropes and ropes of greater diameter *should not* be coiled in this way; alternate procedures are discussed below.

How to Coil Rope

The proper method of making up a coil is to hold the rope in the left hand, about two feet from the end, with the standing part under the thumb. (Southpaws can reverse hands in this operation without affecting the result.) The right hand slides down the standing part about three to four feet, depending on the size of coil desired. The right hand then brings the rope up to the left, laying in a coil and twisting between the thumb and forefinger so that the coil hangs flat. This operation is repeated until the rope is coiled. Often, one end of the rope to be coiled is attached, as in halyards, dock lines, and sheets. The coiling should always start with this end, so that the twist can escape at the free end.

Most lines are tied or hanked one way or another, especially if they are to be stored. The knowledgeable seaman should be familiar with the several standard ways of doing this because it is often necessary to grab a hank of rope, untie it, and pay it out all very quickly. If the rope is hanked in an unfamiliar or haphazard manner, untying it can become time-consuming, and if done hastily can result in a terrible tangle. Practice in hanking and unhanking rope pays off in safe and efficient docking, anchoring, and sailing.

Sheet and dock line coils should not be tied off if these ropes are in use — the delay of untying could slow down urgently needed adjustment.

Finishing off coils is most critical in the case of halyards, as there is no less tractable problem than a knot jammed in the halyard of a sail that must come down. Some sailors try to avoid this issue by stuffing halyards into canvas sacks or boxes — anything can happen in such a rat's nest.

There are two standard ways to finish off halyard coils. One is to reach through the coil and grab the first loop of the halyard (the one next to the cleat). This loop is twisted as it comes through the coil and pushed down on the upper horn of the cleat. I used this method for years but have abandoned it because it chafes a part of the halyard which is under tension when sails are reefed or when the bosun's chair is in use, and also because coils can drop off during rough going. A much better method is to take the last (outside) coil and wrap it *around* the entire coil once, pass it through the top of the coil, and hang it on the cleat or winch (see photo sequence 2). Any chafe that occurs is thus very near the end of the halyard, and this type of hank does not fall off. I do not see that any of the various devices used for holding halyard coils — Velcro strips and shock cords among them — are necessary.

The most widely used method of hanking a coil of rope to be stored is to wrap the end around the coil several times and bring it through the eye at the head of the coil (see photo sequence 3). This works well and provides a free end from which the hank can be hung. I tie such hanks to the hanging-locker bar with clove hitches, which is an excellent way to store ropes and lines. If there is no surplus closet space, cleats can be mounted for this purpose. If this kind of hank is not hung from its end, it tends to loosen.

An excellent way of hanking a coil which will not be hung is to pass the last coil around the hank once or twice and bring the loop through the eye of the coil. The loop is then forced over the top of the coil where it jams in place (see photo sequence 4). It takes some practice to get the loop to come out the right size. I like this method because it never loosens on its own and is quickly undone.

111

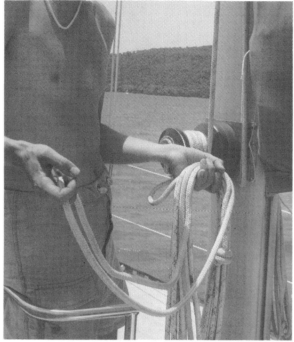

2a

2c

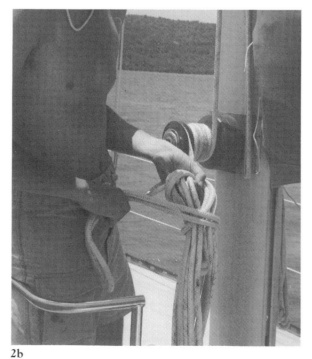

2b

2a. To hank a halyard tail, start at the winch and make a coil.

2b. Wrap the last outside loop around the coil once.

2c. After passing the loop through the top of the hank, hang it on the winch.

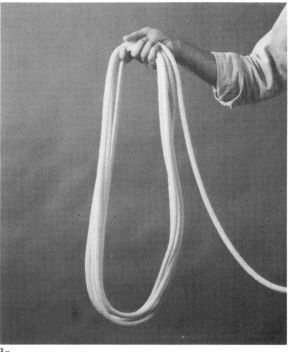

3a

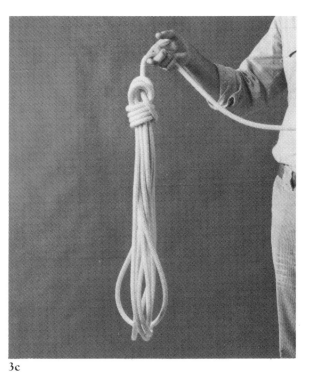

3c

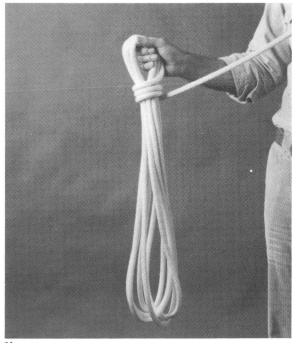

3b

3a. Ready to hank a coil of rope.

3b. Wrap the end around the head of the coil. Continue the wrap a few turns.

3c. The end has been brought through the tail and the hank is finished. It may be hung by clove-hitching the free end to a bar or pin, or belaying to a mast cleat.

4a

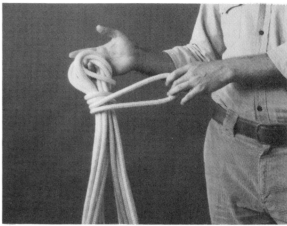

4b

4c

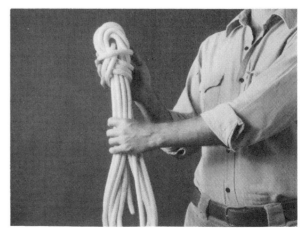

4d

4a. Finishing off a coil that will not be hung. First, take the last loop.

4b. Wrap the loop around the top of the hank several times, then bring the loop up through the eye of the hank.

4c. The loop is ready to be pushed over the top of the hank.

4d. The finished hank.

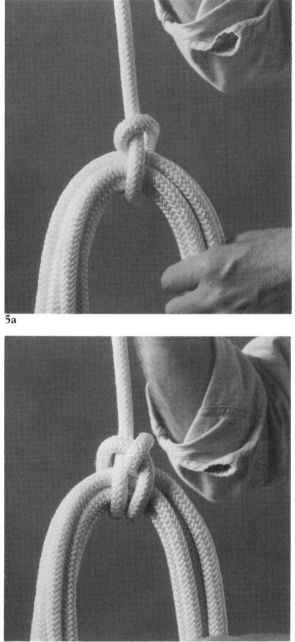

5a

5b

The third standard hanking method is to tie the end around the coil with a few hitches. The most suitable hitches are a half hitch on top of another half hitch. The result resembles a clove hitch except that both parts do not pass under the turn. This kind of hank is most suited to small cordage (see photo sequence 5).

Long lines, such as anchor rodes, and ropes of large diameter in general should not be coiled in a continuous circle or helix. If such a rope is to be laid up on deck and stowed later, the best method is to use the figure-eight pattern (see photo sequence 6). The rope can then be tied off with pieces of small cord, doubled over to make a circular pile, and put away. It is often convenient to lay a rope directly into a small space, such as a bow anchor locker, where a figure eight cannot be laid out. The best method here is to coil circularly until twist is felt in the rope, and then to reverse direction. I keep a few hundred feet of ⅞-inch three-strand nylon rope in CYCLURA's bow stored in this manner and have never had any problems.

A rather different method of storing a long piece of rope is to have a spool mounted so that the rope can be rolled up on it. Hal Roth has such a spool on WHISPER's transom for a stern anchor rode. I have seen a picture of an anchor-rode spool which ran on a shaft screwed into a mast-mounted halyard winch; many other locations are also possible. I have considered such rigs for each of my yachts, but have felt that they offered few advantages. A deck-mounted spool would clutter things up. A spool which had to be carried on deck could be difficult in foul weather, yet a below-deck spool would be inconvenient to coil line onto, probably requiring two people for the job. The reels I have seen which appeared most satisfactory to me are the self-winding ones on some small one-design boats. These could be used for sheets and halyards on many small boats, avoiding confusion and saving labor.

6a

6b

6c

6d

6a. Figure-eight coiling is the only way to keep large line from twisting. If this 100 feet of ⅞-inch nylon rope were coiled in a circle, it would almost certainly hockle when payed out.

6b. To finish off a figure-eight coil, first tie a piece of cord around the top of one loop.

6c. Then fold the loops together, tying the whole bundle together with cord.

6d. The bundle now acts like a single coil and is easy to move and store.

116

Line Storage

The problem of rope storage is seldom considered nowadays, since synthetic fibers have all but eliminated the rot problem. As a result, on many yachts lines are haphazardly shoved into lockers so that considerable time and effort is required to locate a rope suitable for any particular purpose. This is clearly inefficient. As I mentioned above, lines can be hung from bars or cleats. Hooks, pegs, or belaying pins can also be used. If lockers are used, keep dock lines in one, spring lines in another, and so forth.

Coding of Lines

I am convinced that when possible, all lines should be coded. On CYCLURA, all running rigging is white braid, while ground tackle is white twisted. Such coding can save considerable fumbling on dark, wet nights. I may eventually use all eight-plait dock lines. Some European manufacturers sell Dacron braid in several colors so that each piece of running rugging can have its own color code. This may be useful on racers, but on cruisers there is likely to be little confusion among pieces of running rigging.

117

Sweating Up Lines

Sweating is a time-honored way of tightening a line on a cleat. The standing part of the line is pulled sideways — lateral load effect at work again (see page 169) — and released at the same moment that slack is taken up at the cleat. When these actions are properly co-ordinated, considerable tension can be achieved beyond that attainable by simply pulling on the end of the line. This technique can also be used in conjunction with winches, and is quite useful in the case of snubbing winches, where no other mechanical advantage is available. With mast-mounted halyard winches, a bit of sweating can save a trip back to the cockpit for a handle.

I have invented a routine which exerts even greater force than sweating and which has saved me many such trips. I uncleat the halyard and make a loop in its end by letting a bight hang down and wrapping the end over the drum for a few counterclockwise turns. I put a foot in the bight and stand on it, while holding both the end and the standing part of the halyard in my hand. By rocking my body, I can sweat up the halyard as tight as with a single-action winch. I developed this technique when I bought IPHISA, as the previous owner had lost all of the winch handles.

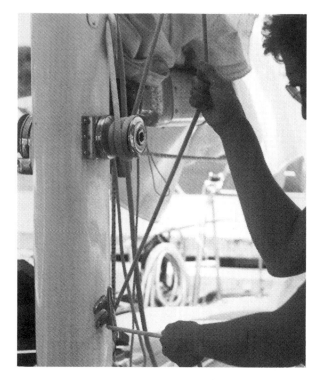

Above: the traditional method of sweating up a halyard.

Below: using body weight and lateral load effect together, it is possible to sweat up lines very tightly.

Open Winches

The simplest form of open winch, the "snubbing winch," is no more than a drum with concave sides that is racheted so that it rotates in one direction only. If we take a line under tension and wrap it around the drum (in the proper direction) and pull on the free end, the drum will rotate and the line will be hauled in. When we stop pulling, the tension on the line will tend to pull the free end back in the direction in which it came, but the drum will not turn in this direction and the friction of the line against the drum will resist the tension. All open winches depend on this friction between the drum and the turns of line around it to counter most or all of the tension on the standing part of the line. If the pull on the free end of the line is substantial, the friction can be increased by adding turns. It should be possible to add turns on a winch until the free ends of the line can be held between two fingers. If the drum of the winch is full of turns and the pull on the free end is still substantial, something is amiss. Either the line is too slippery (due to the nature of the material, such as polypropylene or because it is lubricated) or the winch is too small to deal with the forces generated in the system.

119

The bottom of a winch drum flares out, and the standing part of the line should come on the drum just at this point; the remaining turns wind upward from there. If the bottom turn — the turn that leads to the standing part and is therefore subject to its full tension — "rides up" over turns higher up on the drum, the winch becomes effectively jammed if the tension is great enough to pin the upper turns to the drum.

Such riding turns occur either because the line leads to the drum from an inappropriate angle or because turns were put on the drum while the standing part was slack. If the lead is too low, the turns may jump off the drum; if it is too high, frequent riding turns will result, creating endless havoc. The lead angle can be adjusted by moving blocks about or by changing the location of the winch. To remove a riding turn, it is necessary to relieve the tension on the standing part. This is usually done by attaching a tag line to the standing part (using a rolling hitch) and cranking it in on another winch or with a tackle.

Letting line out (surging) on a winch seems like a straightforward operation but it is potentially dangerous, a fact many people fail to appreciate. If the proper procedure is not followed, one's fingers can get caught up in the turns on the drum and be subjected to great pressure. The critical danger point is where the free end meets the drum. Most winches work in a clockwise rotation so that this point is at the upper-right side of the winch. The free end should be held with the right hand, and the hand should not come closer than within several inches of the drum. The other hand should also be kept away from this point of contact between the free end and the drum. If the line is not payed off the winch smoothly, jerking motions may pull the fingers dangerously close to the

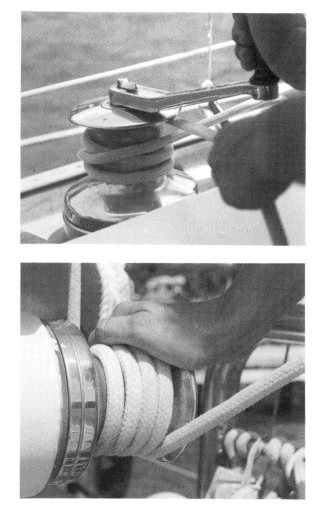

drum. To pay out smoothly, the left hand is laid against the turns on the drum, away from the danger point; the thumb should not be wrapped around the drum or turns. Pressure from the left hand controls the rate at which the turns rotate and the line is payed out. If the line will not pay out smoothly and evenly, a turn is removed from the winch drum. To avoid injury it is necessary to devote full attention to this operation.

Above: riding turns on a cockpit winch.

Below: surging line on a halyard winch.

Single-Action Winches

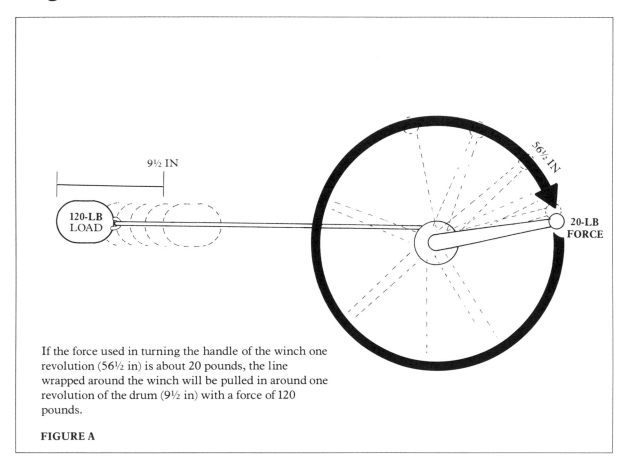

9½ IN

56½ IN

120-LB
LOAD

20-LB
FORCE

If the force used in turning the handle of the winch one revolution (56½ in) is about 20 pounds, the line wrapped around the winch will be pulled in around one revolution of the drum (9½ in) with a force of 120 pounds.

FIGURE A

If we add a simple handle to a snubbing winch, we have made a significant improvement in its usefulness. If the radius of the handle is nine inches and that of the winch drum is 1½ inches (these are typical dimensions), the handle will provide a six-fold mechanical advantage — the force exerted on the standing part of the line will be six times the force used to turn the handle (see figure A). More simply, the handle gives greater purchase in turning the drum. If the handle is racheted so that it bears in the direction that the drum rotates but is free to rotate in the opposite direction, then the handle can always be worked from the most comfortable and mechanically efficient position. (Anyone who has ever used a rachet-mounted socket wrench is familiar with this principle.) This means that the operator of a single-action winch can exert considerably more force in hauling in a line than he could achieve using a simple snubbing winch. The increase in force is roughly proportional to the mechanical advantage provided by the handle. (It is exactly proportional, but other small variables complicate the situation somewhat.)

Geared Winches

The mechanical advantage of winches can be increased either by increasing the ratio between handle length and drum diameter, which is subject to practical limits — handles can become only so long before they become awkward to use and get in the way — or the mechanism can be provided with a system of gears that cause the drum to make fewer revolutions than the handle. With geared winches the mechanical advantage resulting from the handle-to-drum ratio still operates, but it will be multiplied by the ratio by which the gearing reduces the drum rotation. If the handle-to-drum ratio is 6-to-1 as in our previous example, and the gearing causes the drum to make one rotation for each three complete turns of the handle, the total mechanical advantage of the winch is 18-to-1. A force of one "manpower" (about 50 pounds) applied to the handle will result in a line tension of approximately 900 pounds.

Two-Speed Winches

Two-speed winches have two gear ratios. When the handle is rotated in one direction, the winch operates in a high gear, or in ungeared direct action (1-to-1). Rotation of the handle in the other direction engages a lower gear (3-to-1, for example). Since it cannot be internally racheted, the conventional two-speed winch does not offer the advantage of ideal handle position — complete circuits of the handle are required. For this reason the gearing must be somewhat higher than would be required with a single-speed, geared winch. Racheting handles, which are fairly expensive, are available to provide this extra advantage. An internally racheted two-speed winch has recently been developed in

122

Europe, but I have not yet seen one. Three speed winches are available in large sizes and are very expensive. They are useful on big boats for sheeting-in headsails that vary greatly in size.

Winches with mechanical advantages of up to 60-to-1 are commonly available, and winches with much greater ratios are made, raising once again the issue of safety around heavily loaded ropes.

It is important to note that many modest sized single-action winches have mechanical advantages sufficient to exceed the working load of ⅜-inch yacht braid. Considerable damage can be done by the forces generated by winches — ropes can be broken, perhaps causing injury; sails can be torn; and structural damage can be done to the boat itself. The adage, frequently heard from racers, that winches should be as large as one can afford, is simply not true. Sturdy fittings are desirable, but oversized winches, capable of destructive loads, are not. Do not install winches capable of overloading their mountings or the sheets and sails trimmed. I have been on boats whose sheet winches flexed the cockpit combings, which must soon result in failure through fatigue.

Several years ago I was involved in an operation which would now strike me as hairbrained on this account. After a bit of swimming to bring a skipper's wife and children safely ashore, I found myself helping him winch his 33-foot sloop off a lee beach in the middle of a dark, wet, stormy night. The operation depended on a 600-foot piece of 1-inch nylon rope, which had been led to a breakwater. We led this rope through a bow chock and were cranking it strenuously on both large cockpit winches. I do not know what the stress on the rope was, but we were working very hard and I distinctly remember that the rope looked long-jawed. It was certainly under considerable tension, because as the hull finally floated free on a wave crest, it shot forward quite unsluggishly. If the other end had come loose we both could easily have been killed.

Self-Tailing Winches

The major recent development in winches is the addition of a device to tail (feed off) line as the winch is cranked, so that the operator is relieved of the necessity of handling the lines. Line is stripped off the top of the drum by a metal finger-guide and held between a spring-loaded plate and the upper flange of the drum. The designs in which the pressure plate rotates with the drum, rather than being immobile, appear to work the best. To use the self-tailing feature (such winches can also be used in the hand-tailing mode) several turns must be taken on the drum, because the pressure plate functions best under light line load. With heavy load and few turns, the line will either be damaged by the jamming device or jump out. With the drum full of turns, the line is led over the guide and a turn is taken under the pressure plate. Once the line is jammed in the self-tailing device, it can be ignored. The winch is cranked with a handle in the usual way. Self-tailing winches are also self-cleating — the free end of the line does not have to be secured in any other way (see photo sequence 7).

I have had complete success with CYCLURA's self-tailing winches (in spite of disparaging remarks from many other yachtsmen). All seven of my winches are self-tailers, and I have no nearby cleats as back-up. The usual concern is that the self-tailing device cannot be trusted to hold line as well as a cleat. I have never had a line fall loose, including

the staysail halyard which on one voyage was not touched between raising in Newport and lowering in St. Thomas, 12 days later.

Self-tailing winches are a boon to single-hand sailors and were seen on most yachts competing in the latest OSTAR and the Route du Rhum. I can tack my 40-foot cutter, with two sets of sheets and running backstays, with little more trouble than what my 32-foot sloop IPHISA gave me, thanks to these winches. I prefer them for other kinds of sailing as well.

7a

7b

7a. Two turns on a self-tailing winch. This is the best way to haul a sheet by hand.

7b. To crank the winch in self-tailing mode, fill the drum with turns and lead the line over the guide.

7c. Lead the line around the cleating mechanism and seat it with a light yank.

7d. Cranking the self-tailing winch.

7c

7d

Reel Halyard Winches

Here is a line-handling device to stay away from. For many decades of yachting, the reel-type halyard winch was the device used for handling wire-cable main halyards because there was no decent way to attach a rope tail to the wire cable. The problem with the reel halyard winch is that it occasionally gets out of control. A winch handle is used to wind the wire cable around a drum, which is racheted so as to be free to rotate clockwise on a base plate. The halyard is set up by cranking the handle. It is released by releasing the brake (usually a band clutch) which allows the base plate to freewheel along with the reel and, if it has not been removed, the handle. Halyard tension can cause the whole assembly to spin like a top. Arms and skulls have been broken by spinning handles on reel-type winches. Many prudent yachtsmen, myself included, will not have such winches aboard. They are obsolete today in any case, as yacht braid can be successfully spliced to 7x19 wire cable and the tail winched satisfactorily in open winches.

Sheet Stoppers

The main application of sheet (and halyard) stoppers is to lead more than one line to a winch. One obvious advantage in reducing the number of winches is economy, but the saving in weight and clutter is probably more important. Often, there is just no other place to put another winch, and one large winch may well be more desirable than two smaller ones, even at the same cost. I have several stoppers on CYCLURA and have plans to install more. Both mainsheet and main halyard lead to a single winch on the cabin top, and each has a stopper. While the main is being hoisted there is little tension on the sheet — the sheet stopper holds it in place, and it can quickly be adjusted. When the halyard is set up, it is set in its stopper and the turns taken off the winch, which is then used for the sheet. To release the halyard, it is necessary to take the sheet off the winch and to take up the halyard tension before the stopper can be released. In practice, there is virtually no conflict between the winching requirements of sheet and halyard for a given sail.

On the other side of the cabin top, a single winch is used for the staysail halyard. If a single-sheet, self-tacking staysail were set, its sheet could be led to the same winch. I prefer the more efficient double-sheeted, overlapping type of staysail, which is trimmed with secondary cockpit winches. I plan to lead my mainsail reefing-clew pennants to the staysail halyard winch eventually, because I like to minimize the time spent out of the cockpit in rough weather; four stoppers will be required to effect this rig. I also plan to install stoppers on the mast to handle the two jib halyards with a single winch. At present, the secondary jib halyard is tied off as a spare.

The limitation of all existing stopper designs with which I am familiar is that the lines cannot usually all be led true to the winch. Some degree of turn is usually necessary at the stopper in most installations, and this turn is taken across polished metal generating considerable friction when high tension is applied, such as with the halyard on CYCLURA's 430-square-foot mainsail. The design problem appears to be that all of the manufacturers are attempting to sell a module which can be stacked to handle any given number of lines, rather than designing a device which does a proper job of stopping and leading a given number of lines to a winch.

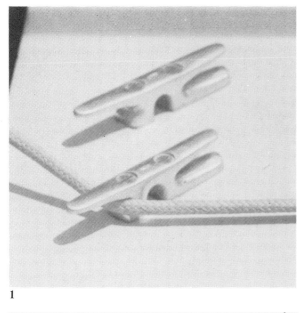

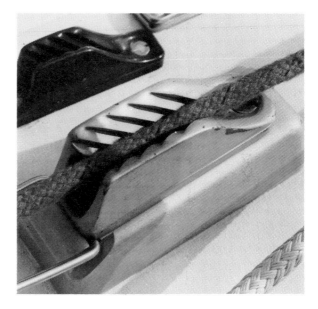

1

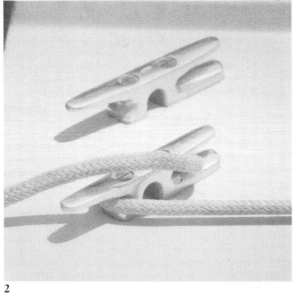

2

Jam Cleats and Cam Cleats

These devices offer quick ways of stopping or holding a line under tension. The jam cleat, in its various forms, works by wedging the line in a V-shaped channel, while the cam cleat has a pair of hinged jaws which bear on the line. Both cause considerably more chafe than does a sheet stopper. They are most useful on tackles and light control lines because under heavy load both are difficult to disengage. In both cases the angle of the free end is adjusted in order to engage or free the line; the cleat must be positioned in such a way that this adjustment can be readily done. I have occasionally rigged boom vangs with the cam cleat near the deck so that it was almost impossible to disengage. It is usually possible to handle such a boom vang from the cockpit if the cam cleat is at the upper end. Some of the less expensive fiddle blocks for boom vangs have a "V" groove which serves as a jam cleat. Under tension, these can be very difficult to disengage and can cause considerable damage to the rope.

Above: belaying a line on a jam cleat.

1. The line crosses the cleat on the open end.

2. The line is then brought around and pulled into the "V" groove.

Right: Clamcleat, a patented jam cleat. For a picture of a cam cleat, see page 151.

127

Blocks

Blocks serve two related purposes. One is to change the direction of a line, and the other is to gain mechanical advantage by rigging tackles. The need to change lead angles is obvious enough. A halyard has to go to the top of a mast and then pass through a block before coming back down. A headsail sheet must leave the clew at a particular angle to trim the sail and arrive at a winch at another angle for the winch to function properly. Blocks provide a relatively efficient and friction-free way for these lines to turn their corners in changing direction.

Tackles

A tackle is an arrangement of line and two or more blocks that applies a mechanical advantage. Before the widespread use of winches, tackles were the general means of applying mechanical advantage in hauling lines. Today, the use of tackles is limited to a relatively small number of tasks — primarily the handling of mainsheets, boom vangs, down- and outhauls, and similar applications.

The mechanical advantage of a tackle is determined by the number of parts of line (strands) pulling on the movable block—a three-part tackle provides a 3-to-1 advantage; a five-part tackle, 5-to-1, etc. For each length that the fall (free end of the line) is pulled, the movable block will move that distance divided by the number of parts: if you pull the fall on a four-part tackle one foot, the block will move three inches. If you need to move the block one foot with a five-part tackle, you will have to pull five feet on the fall. Herein lies the major disadvantage of tackles: if the distance you need to move the block is substantial, especially if it is a tackle of many

Vang tackle mounted on a track.

parts, the lengths of line you must deal with can become horrendously long. By contrast, the mechanical advantage supplied by a winch does not affect the lengths of your lines. Winches are also available in a much greater range of mechanical advantages; the practical limit with tackles is a mechanical advantage of 8-to-1. So tackles are used now in situations in which the disadvantage is traded off against some advantage or necessity. In the case of mainsheet tackles, the advantage gained is that the load of the mainsail can be distributed by this means among several strands of relatively light, easy-to-handle line rather than a single heavier one. Since fairly complex lead angle problems are

128

1

2

also involved here, the tackle is a natural solution.

The most widely used type of mainsheet tackle has a cam cleat on the lower block so that line does not lead to any winch or deck cleat. This is usually attached to a traveler car. If, instead of the cam cleat, the fall is led to a deck block, tension on this part will not be in the same direction as the rest of the tackle and will reduce the effectiveness of the traveler in controlling sail shape. The solution I have used on CYCLURA so that I could lead the fall to a winch was to run it forward, under the boom, to a block mounted under the gooseneck, and then to a deck block. Since the fall pivots at the same point as the boom, it has no effect on the boom position.

Dozens of mainsheet tackle arrangements have been devised, incorporating many ingenious features. A number of these provide some traveler effect without an actual traveler. One, shown in photo 2 (left), has the advantage that the sheet has two ends, either of which can be trimmed.

Another advantage that tackles can provide is that they can be easily moved or relocated, whereas winches are of necessity fixed. This makes them useful in boom vangs and similar applications. Boom vangs are the general-purpose tackles of our time. Most have a cleating mechanism so that they do not have to be choked (tying the fall to the other parts) and they can be attached almost anywhere with their snap-shackle ends.

1. A four-part mainsheet tackle which leads forward to the gooseneck and then back to a deck cleat.

2. An unusual mainsheet tackle arrangement providing a 6-to-1 mechanical advantage and trimming from either side.

Tackle on a dinghy davit.

In addition to their application as vangs, tackles can be rigged for a multitude of other purposes, from bringing the dinghy aboard to hauling a halyard down so as to remove a riding turn from its winch. Several such tackles would be invaluable in case of dismasting. Once the spar is down, the biggest danger is that it will do additional damage by flailing about. The first order of business is to tie it firmly to the hull, which can be done fairly rapidly by snapping on vangs and hauling in.

Roller-furling jib halyards use two- to three-part tackles because great headstay tension is required to keep the sail from sagging. A one-part halyard would have to be very heavy to handle this tension, and a larger-than-usual winch would be required to trim it. Both problems are solved with a two- or three-part halyard tackle. Such halyards used to be used for mainsails as well. Trimming halyards with winches greatly reduces their length — 50 feet of halyard tail is easier to coil than 100 or 150 feet needed for a two- or three-part halyard.

Spanish Windlass

Eventually, a tackle will not be available when needed. This is almost inevitable in sorting things out after dismasting, where a baker's dozen of tackles would come in handy. The Spanish windlass (which is no more than a tourniquet on a grand scale) is a useful substitute. All that is involved is wrapping a length of rope around two objects which are to be drawn together. A handle of some sort is used to twist the several parts of the rope, and considerable tension can be exerted; the mechanical advantage depends on the length of the handle.

Two-by-four lumber and ½-inch rope make a good Spanish windlass.

Spanish windlasses can be used to firmly lash down a heavy object, such as a 55-gallon drum or an outboard motor that is in danger of breaking loose. The greatest limitation of this device is that it is not effective in drawing things together by more than half the distance separating them. A tackle, in contrast, maintains full efficiency until the blocks collide. Of course another, smaller Spanish windlass can be rigged alongside the one which has bottomed out.

I n this chapter we will examine the various methods (aside from knotting and splicing) by which the ends of rigging materials are joined or attached. These can be broken down into two broad groups: systems of attaching formed terminals, such as eyes or forks, to the ends of rigging members; and a method of fastening wire cables around thimbles to make eyes that can in turn be attached to other fittings — the second being a mechanical substitute for the eye splice.

The use of formed terminals is essential with rod rigging and fairly essential with 1x19 wire cable and with certain fiber ropes that cannot be spliced, knotted, or otherwise bent. With 7x7 cable, terminals often work well, though they are certainly not essential. Attaching 7x19 cable generally works better with the splice-substitute method.

Swaged Fittings

The most widely used means of attaching terminals to the ends of 1x19 wire is swaging — it is inexpensive (in comparison with all but thimble ends), lightweight, and elegant in appearance. The fittings used incorporate a long tube into which the wire end is inserted; then, high mechanical pressure is used to compress the tube around the wire, so that the two are securely joined. The walls of the tube actually get molded around the wire as if the fitting were clay. This system, originally developed for aircraft control cables, was first used in yacht rigging after World War II.

Several types and a complete range of sizes of swage-on fittings are available. Forks, eyes, and studs which thread directly into turnbuckles are the basic configurations. Swage-on fittings are available in types 303, 304, and 316 stainless steel. Types 316 and 304, having superior corrosion resistance and a longer lifespan, are most desirable. Type 303, used to reduce machining costs and so to increase profit margins, is not very corrosion-resistant.

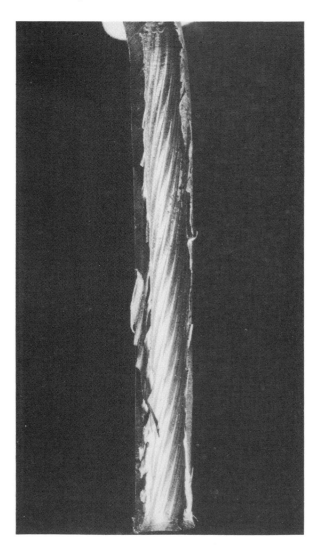

Longitudinal section of a swaged fitting, in which the impressions of the cable wires can be seen clearly.

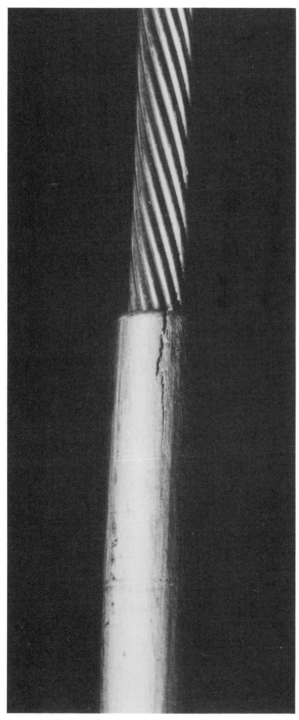

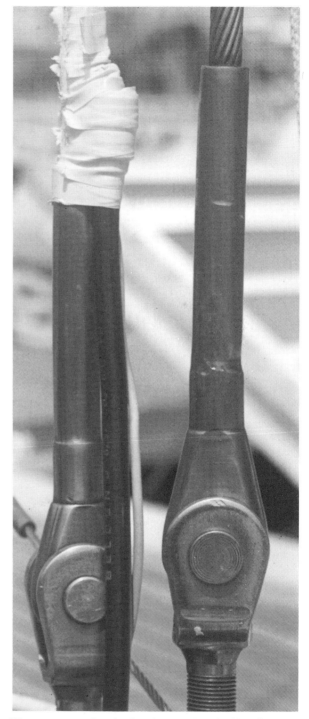

Swaged fitting showing stress cracks.   Kearney swaged ends showing marks of roller dies.

The Kearney swaging machine.

Two types of swaging machines are used by yacht-riggers — the Kearney and the rotary swaging machine. The Kearney machine rolls the fitting between two rotary dies. On the first pass, the fitting acquires an elliptical section. The second pass, made at 90° to the first, restores the circular section. (Kearney-swaged fittings can be distinguished by longitudinal ridges caused by the edges of the rolling dies.) The Kearney is widely used because it is much less expensive than the rotary swaging machine. However, a rotary-swaged fitting is much smoother. The rotary has a split tubular die which revolves around the fitting while being pressed inward.

The disadvantages of tubular swage-on fittings are twofold: first, they are more subject to failure than any other terminal fitting. The pressure-rolling process creates small cracks on the inner surface of the bore. Under load, these cracks widen slowly until they surface on the exterior of the fitting. For this reason, swaged ends should be examined regularly and replaced as soon as the smallest crack is evident. The second disadvantage is that if the swaged terminal is to be scrapped, several inches of wire cable must be sacrificed with it.

All cruising yachts with swaged standing rigging should carry a back-up system to replace cracked fittings. One way is to have spares made up; on a standard sloop you will need one stay — two if the forestay and backstay are of very different lengths — and one upper shroud and one lower shroud. I prefer to carry everything needed to slowly convert to another type of terminal.

136

Screw-On Terminals

A 1x19 cable lifeline connected to a shroud with a cable clamp mounted in a screw-on fork terminal.

Screw-on terminals are the choice do-it-yourself system for 1x19 rigging. The great advantage of the screw-on terminals made by Norseman, STA-LOK, and Loos is that installation takes no more than a few minutes' work with wrenches, and used on wire, these terminals are as strong as the cable. The principle of operation is entirely mechanical and quite simple. The wire end is passed through a bore with tight clearance which then widens conically. The outer strands of the wire are unlaid and a wedge piece is threaded over the core strands. After the outer strands are relaid over the wedge, the bore fitting is brought down over the swollen wire end and a screw fitting (with eye, fork, or stud) presses the wire into the conical bore. The terminals are reuseable with replacement wedges.

The design of the STA-LOK terminals is superior to that of the Norseman and Loos, which are identical. The bending of the strand ends is simpler and faster in the STA-LOK — it's accomplished as the fitting is screwed together. With the Norseman and Loos terminals, the strand ends must be bent with pliers before the end part is screwed on.

Secondly, the STA-LOK arrangement is fail-safe, while the Norseman and Loos are not. The bore fitting of the STA-LOK has a male thread which screws into the female thread in the end fitting, in contrast to the other design, which has the female thread on the bore fitting. A crack in the bore fitting will be contained by the end fitting in the STA-LOK, but not in the Norseman or Loos terminals.

And last of all, all parts of the STA-LOK terminals are type 316 stainless, while the Norseman and Loos are 303, with a soft metal cone. The latter two are susceptible to electrolysis (which can result in the explosion of the eye); the STA-LOK is not.

As mentioned, screw-on terminals can be reused if the wedges are replaced each time. Wedges are available for use on 1x19, 7x7, and 7x19 wire. A recent innovation from STA-LOK is a wedge for rod rigging, which is threaded on. This is an appealing arrangement, because, substituting the appropriate wedge, the rod can easily be replaced with wire in case of failure. All other methods of attaching rod rigging make replacement with wire complicated and expensive. I do, however, think that this system for rod rigging needs additional testing.

Terminals for Rope

A few types of low-stretch braided ropes are unspliceable. A wedge-type terminal is the common method of attaching a halyard made of this type of rope to the jib head. In the terminals I have seen, the rope end is inserted into a tubular piece with a flared or conical interior. A wedge is then pushed into the rope end and a screw-in piston locks the assembly together. The piston parts (fitting ends) are available as eyes or with snap shackles. This kind of gear is expensive.

Poured Terminals

So-called "poured terminals," the original wire cable terminals, are still in use. The principle is very simple. The end of the cable is inserted into the conical bore of the fitting (cast bronze sockets are the best type), the wire is unlaid for the length of the bore, and the ends are held captive in a mass of metal, poured into the socket in molten state.

The appearance of poured terminals is rather large and clunky — a factor that limits their use on modern-looking yachts. They are an excellent, economical choice for rerigging large old-fashioned boats, however; their cost is about half that of screw-on terminals (although they do require more effort and paraphernalia to install).

As with any soldering operation, it is important that the parts be clean. The cable end is first degreased with kerosene or other solvent and wiped dry. The end is then pushed through the socket and unlaid a length equal to that of the socket cavity. The frayed end is dipped in dilute muriatic acid for a minute and then thoroughly rinsed with water. When everything is dry, the frayed end is pulled back into the socket and the socket is held in a vise so that solder can be poured in. The best results will be obtained if the socket and wire are heated with a torch before pouring. The desired temperature is slightly above the melting point of the solder, which can be determined by putting a drop of solder on the wire ends and observing when it melts. At this point, solder is poured in with a ladle, accompanied by light tapping around the socket, which helps to move the solder throughout the cavity. If excessive solder leaks from the socket during pouring, seal it with a short wire whipping on the cable just where it enters the socket.

1x19 wire cable held in a poured terminal.

Glued Terminals

A recent innovation is the glued terminal (trade-named Castlok) in which epoxy takes the place of solder in poured terminals. These terminals are very strong and durable.

The installation is straightforward. The wire cable end is degreased. After being passed through the tubular fitting, the cable is unlaid for a few turns and then withdrawn into the tubular part. A measured amount of epoxy is provided in a two-compartment plastic bag. Mixing is done by massaging the bag, which is then pierced, and the epoxy is slowly poured into the fitting. When the tubular part is filled with epoxy, the fitting is sealed with a threaded plug, which carries the eye, fork, or stud.

Tests published by *Motor Boating and Sailing* magazine show that Castlok terminals are stronger than the wire cable they are attached to. (The same is also true of screw-on terminals and probably of poured terminals.) I have two reservations. First, they are comparatively inconvenient in terms of installation. Due to set-up time, rigging must be cut to length and made up the day before it is to be installed. With most other types of terminals, installation can follow fabrication immediately. Second, I am reluctant to trust my safety to glues of any kind. My experience with many types over several years' work on houses, boats, cars, and scientific apparatus indicates that glues are not consistently reliable. There are too many variables of temperature, humidity, mixing, and other unknown factors that may conspire to make any glue fail to set up properly. This may not be the case with the materials provided for installing this kind of terminal, but I know that in a blow I would worry about their sturdiness.

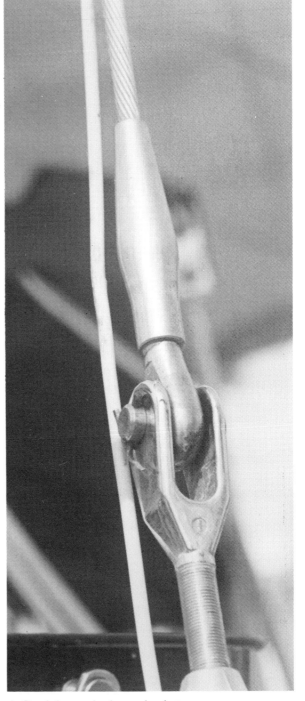

A Castlok terminal on a backstay.

Rope Clips

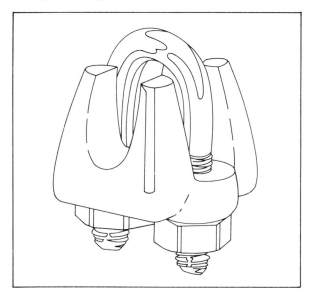

A loop can be made in 1 x 19 or other wire cable with rope clips, also known as cable clamps, which are merely U-bolts with special clamp fittings. At least three of these should be used for a strong loop, two with the bolt-side positioned on the standing part and one positioned in the opposite direction. Such loops are strong and useful for emergency repairs, but so unsightly and prone to snagging that they are not suitable for normal standing rigging use.

Sleeve Swaging

My 32-foot sloop IPHISA was rigged with 7 x 19 wire cable, with thimble ends attached with Nicopress sleeves. The elasticity of the 7 x 19 cable caused some initial problems with the rig, but after eight years of tropical service, the sleeves were still sound. This kind of end treatment is durable and far less expensive than any other. It is an

excellent choice for the economy-minded.

The system consists of copper sleeves, sometimes zinc-coated, that are pressed around the cable with a bolt cutter fitted with special jaws. Loos & Co., which manufactures the Locolok brand of sleeve swager, claims that oval sleeves (those designed to join two cables) will "support a greater load than the rated breaking strength of 7 x 7 and 7 x 19 cable."

The basic procedure for installing swaged sleeves is very simple. The cable is cut clean and passed through the sleeve, around the thimble, and back through the sleeve. Careful adjustment and alignment of all parts is fairly critical for good results, and it may take a little while to get the knack of leaving the right amount of slack for the sleeves to take up on expansion.

If your sleeve has room for three presses, the first press should be in the middle. The cut end of the cable should be protruding about ⅛ inch before crimping (pressing), and the loop around the thimble should not be very tight initially. Expansion of the sleeve on crimping will snug up the fit of the cable around the thimble and will cover the cut cable end. If you are using a two-press sleeve, set up the loop around the thimble fairly tightly, making the first press near the thimble.

Careful examination of your early attempts will help you to determine what adjustments are necessary to make the loops come out at the right tension and have the cut ends of the cable come out even with the sleeve ends. At the proper tension the thimble should just be able to move within the loop.

I also used Nicopress sleeves to install CYCLURA's lifelines. They do an excellent job of securing plastic-coated 7 x 7 cable.

Above: making a sleeve-swaged eye.

Below: halyard ends, two Nicopressed and one with an unserved splice. Note how the Nicopress connections are pressed down on the thimbles and how, as a result, the cable does not lead fair. This is caused by putting the sleeves too close to the thimbles before crimping.

Rod Terminals

A cold-head turnbuckle ready for final assembly.

There are three types of terminals compatible with rod rigging. The rod end can be knurled or threaded and swaged into the same kind of tubular fitting used for wire cable. But, since the swage-on fittings themselves are the weak link in all swaged terminal systems, it seems a particularly unsuitable solution for rod, which is essentially a permanent rigging material.

Rod can also be attached with mechanical (screw-on) terminals using special conical threaded wedges developed for this purpose.

The third system, developed especially for rod rigging by Navtec, Inc., is a process known as "cold-heading." Specially designed fittings, bored to the diameter of the rod, are slipped over the rod ends which are then pressed by machine into a knob about twice the diameter of the rod, preventing the fittings from escaping. The process in no way weakens the rod. Several different types of cold-head fittings are manufactured by Navtec.

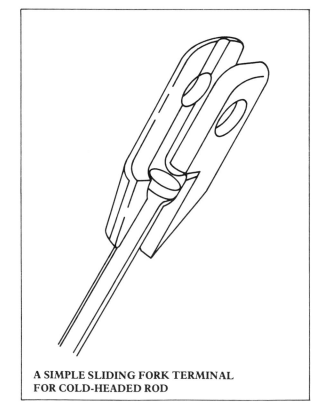

A SIMPLE SLIDING FORK TERMINAL FOR COLD-HEADED ROD

Conclusion

As we have seen, quite a number of methods of attaching standing and running rigging are available. I do not intend to review the attendant advantages and disadvantages in detail, just to underscore some broad points.

Tubular swage-on terminals, regardless of what material they are being attached to and regardless of whether Kearney or rotary swages are used, are apt to develop cracks and fail. The tradeoff for their availability, economy, and ease of installation is vigilance in maintenance. They will have to be inspected regularly and carefully and rigging replaced periodically when they fail.

Mechanical end terminals, while comparatively expensive, are extremely reliable. They offer compatibility with the greatest number of rigging materials. This makes them very useful in various types of emergency repair situations, and makes it possible to use the same terminals when changing over from one type of rigging to another.

Rod rigging with cold-head fittings would seem to be a durable and reliable system, but it has one major drawback: it is repairable only with the proper machinery, so in any long-distance cruising situation, some sort of a back-up system would have to be carried.

Thimble ends fastened with swaged sleeves are economical, easy to make, and quite durable. One can easily keep on board all the tools and materials necessary for fabrication and repair. The tradeoff in this system is dealing with the less-than-ideal properties of 7 x 19 cable as material for standing rigging.

Above: pressing in the pin that locks screw-assembled cold-head terminals for rod.

Below: a cold-head eye terminal attached to a toggle. Rod terminals should be toggled to prevent fatigue.

**Chapter 7
Hardware**

Much of classic marlinspike practice has been superseded by the use of modern nautical hardware. We now use turnbuckles instead of deadeyes and lanyards, terminals instead of splices, and even hydraulic cylinders rather than tackles in some cases. Other items of hardware — blocks and cleats, for example — have been associated with marlinspike from time immemorial. My purpose in this chapter is to review this marlinspike hardware, both the newfangled and the traditional, in an attempt to equip the reader with most of the information required to rig a boat.

The hardware catalogues of the various manufacturers make an impressive array in a file, but the number of basic hardware designs is actually fairly limited. Most of the diversity is in style of appearance and in quality of materials. Prices vary roughly in proportion to quality and to some extent in proportion to the reputation of the brand name. It is common practice today to issue catalogues annually, with so-called "new" items conspicuously marked. There is clearly considerable expenditure on updating designs for marketing rather than functional reasons. One result of this is that some of the "new" items function less well than the common old ones they replace. Another is that some very basic pieces of hardware have become unavailable through lack of demand. For this reason, some comments on fabrication of custom fittings are in order.

Cleats

There is an enormous market for cleats. Even the smallest yacht stores usually stock several lines, offering a variety of designs and materials in the usual six- to eight-inch sizes (size refers to overall length between the tips of the horns).

Virtually all cleats available in stores and catalogues are metal; wooden cleats are, nonetheless, practical and inexpensive. The great drawback of wooden cleats, or anything else wooden on deck, is maintenance. The best wood for cleats is probably locust, but it checks (cracks) badly if not sealed several times a year. Teak is essentially maintenance-free, but without regular sealing it looks bad. Stainless steel cleats are at the other end of the durability spectrum, requiring virtually no maintenance. Bronze is also maintenance-free, but looks much better when polished. High-quality anodized aluminum cleats give good maintenance-free service, but others of lower quality pit or corrode very badly. The quality of chromed bronze cleats is also quite variable — when they are good, they are on a par with good stainless; when they are bad, they are awful. White metal and galvanized iron or steel have no place on the deck of a modern yacht; plastic cleats are only useable for the lightest service, such as flag halyards.

Most features of cleat design are not functional, but decorative. There should be no radius on any cleat which is less than the diameter of the largest rope to be belayed — a criterion that disqualifies the overwhelming majority of designs. For deck use — with anchor rodes and dock lines — I see nothing better than the classic "hollow" cleat. Even some of these, however, have been "improved" by adding corners around the base. These corners will chafe ropes. With stainless steel or unplated bronze cleats, the corners can be filed off. If a file is taken to chromed or anodized cleats, however, they will have to be recoated. The appeal of the hollow cleat is that a line can be surged with one turn under the aft horn or with two turns, one under each horn, yet the line still leads fairly and does not jam. With many other designs, smooth surging is essentially impossible.

A common mistake is to install cleats that are too small for the duty they are called upon to perform. The motivation here must be to save money or reduce deck clutter; some all-out racers may also be concerned about weight. Since an undersize cleat is almost useless, it is better to have fewer and larger cleats. Every yacht needs one heavy-duty line attachment on the bow. If this is a cleat, it should be as large as can be comfortably accommodated, because there is no way

of knowing the size of a towline or mooring that may be used in an emergency. Any boat with a foredeck can take an eight-inch cleat; ten-inch cleats will fit on 20- to 30-footers; and 12-inch and larger cleats should be mounted on yachts above 30 feet overall. At the lower end of these ranges, a single cleat mounted on the midline is probably adequate. With hollow cleats, the length of the cleat divided by 16 gives the maximum size rope that can be easily handled. Thus, ½-inch rope fits an eight-inch cleat, a six-inch cleat is limited to ⅜-inch rope, ⅝-inch rope goes on ten-inch cleats, and ¾-inch rope on twelve-inch cleats. Of course, such limits are not absolute and bigger ropes can be handled, although inefficiently, if need be. On CYCLURA's 12-inchers, it is barely possible to belay and impossible to surge ⅞-inch nylon anchor rode that has hardened as a result of immersion; I normally use the windlass for such work anyway. One-inch line probably could not be belayed on these cleats at all, but attachment could be made by putting a loop over the aft horn.

Much cleat "improvement" has focused on streamlining. This has been counterproductive, because lowering the horns reduces the facility with which rope can be passed under. Deck cleats should readily accept at least two turns of the largest rope routinely used. Streamlining is more desirable for cleats mounted on masts and booms, but this can also be counterproductive. It is desirable to be able to sweat up tension on most lines that lead to spar-mounted cleats (see Chapter 5), and this is often impossible on low-profile, streamlined models. It is essential to have a cleat under which a turn will run smoothly.

Frequently, the most practical place to mount a large deck cleat, such as in the middle of the foredeck, is also a place where it

will regularly interfere with running rigging. One way around this problem, rather than to move the cleat, is to isolate it from the sheets; I have seen two neat ways of doing this. Blocks of wood can be fashioned so that they jam under each cleat horn, fairing in the cleat to the deck. These blocks can be connected by shock cords running parallel to the cleat, as shown in the photograph above.

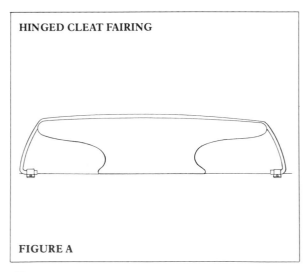

HINGED CLEAT FAIRING

FIGURE A

The same effect can be achieved with a frame made from stainless steel bar stock, hinged on the midline of the cleat, which snaps into a groove on the top of the cleat, closing off the horns when the cleat is idle. This type of cleat guard, or fairing, is shown in the accompanying diagram (see figure A). Unfortunately, the product is not widely distributed, so it most probably will have to be custom fabricated. This at least has the advantage of leaving one free to choose any cleat.

A recent innovation is a stainless steel bar bent into the silhouette of a cleat and hinged on a deck plate. The cleat shape is utterly unfunctional and the device is definitely not an improvement over the cleat it is supposed to replace, or even over a deck ring, which it more closely resembles. In fact, the deck ring is preferable in that it will lie flush when idle. Another innovation, with which I have more sympathy, is the track-mounted cleat. These would provide an ideal way to rig spring lines on boats with rail-mounted tracks, eliminating chocks.

148

Windlasses

On all yachts 40 feet or longer that anchor regularly and on ocean cruisers over 30 feet, an anchor windlass is essential. Windlasses are a desirable luxury on smaller yachts. Without a windlass, handling anchor chain is an ordeal. I have hauled a lot of chain by hand and using cockpit winches, experiences I do not wish to repeat. There are three sources of windlass power on yachts: hydraulic, electric, and human. My experiences with electric windlasses convince me that they have almost insuperable shortcomings. I hear good things about hydraulic windlasses, but I have never used one. When I bought IPHISA, her three-year-old open-gear windlass was frozen solid. I replaced it with a single-speed Simpson Lawrence manual windlass, which worked beautifully. On CYCLURA, I have mounted the two-speed manual windlass of the same make, and I am completely satisfied with it. I recently saw a new model that incorporates a counter, resembling that on a tape recorder, measur-

ing the length of chain let out; this is a useful feature.

Manual windlasses are operated by pumping a handle. The gear ratio or ratios are important — if too high, many light strokes are required to make a little progress, and if too low, resistance on the handle can be tiring. Fortunately, manufacturers are aware of this and scale their windlasses to suit boats of given size ranges.

Chain is let out on manual and most other windlasses by loosening a clutch. On some models, including the Simpson Lawrence types I am most familiar with, the clutch is unscrewed against chain tension and, if the clutch is very tight, the chain is hauled instead of the clutch being unscrewed. This problem is solved by a routine of freezing the chain gypsy with a cog while unscrewing the clutch, then cranking the gypsy in slightly to remove the cog, and finally operating the clutch. If the clutch is left screwed tight for extended periods, it is likely to freeze. I leave mine unscrewed but with the cog set and the chain held by a spring line.

Even though I would not have other than a manual windlass on a yacht of mine, I envy those who can afford the luxury of power windlasses (not so much of their purchase as of their maintenance). Hauling in anchors with CYCLURA's windlass is not a terrible chore, but power windlasses can be used for many other things. Foremost among these is hauling up bosun's chairs, a task that has given me many fine workouts. A boat with a power windlass should be rigged so all halyards can be led to the windlass drum. Even if you choose not to use it routinely, eventually it will be more than a convenience, perhaps even making possible a fast single-handed boat-saving getaway.

Posts

The Samson post is a very practical foredeck fixture. Securely installed, stepped on the stem, and braced with deck partners, it provides a solid point of attachment often lacking on yachts. Most yachts do not have any reliable fitting to which a heavy hawser could be attached for towing. A keel-stepped mast is often reliable, but the strength of many extruded masts is inadequate for this taxing service. Deck-stepped masts should *never* be used as a hold-fast, because the attachment to the deck, and most likely the deck itself, has very low shear strength. Thus, without a Samson post, there may not be any place to attach a towline that would be very heavily loaded.

Samson posts should never be of less than four-inch-square section and should always be made of very strong and durable wood, chosen for its straight grain. Locust, white oak, ash, and teak are the preferred woods. The essential qualities are shear strength, good weathering, and a close grain that

will not chafe rope, even after being chafed by chain. The size of Samson posts should be increased in proportion to the size of the yacht. One square inch of section per ton of yacht displacement should be adequate for posts of very strong wood. The end grain of posts is exposed and must be protected. A cast bronze cap cemented on with epoxy is the best way of doing this. Wood sealer regularly applied also works. The vertical edges of Samson posts should be rounded to one-inch radii.

Chain can be belayed on a Samson post by piling on several turns. It is very useful to have a Samson post forward of a windlass; when there is any problem with the windlass, or when the clutch is unscrewed while at anchor, the chain can be left on the post. Rope of any size up to about two-inch diameter can be belayed with the tugman's hitch. A rod is sometimes driven through posts for belaying ropes as if on the horns of a cleat. There is no advantage to such rods; they weaken the post.

Cam Cleats

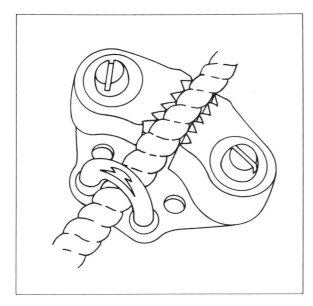

Cam cleats are handy for stopping lines pulled by hand. Spring-loaded toothed jaws grip the line when it is pressed down between them. One model has a release mechanism that is actuated by downward line pressure, while the rest release by pulling the line out of the jaws. The limitation of such cleats is that the line will be damaged and hard to release if load exceeds about 50 pounds. Cam cleats are often found on mainsheet, boom downhaul, and vang tackles. Such tackles are usually three- or four-part and rove with ⅜- or ½-inch rope. The rope cannot usually (and should not) be led to a winch for extra purchase, because the cam cleat will jam under high load, damaging the rope and becoming difficult or impossible to disengage. CYCLURA does not have a cam cleat on her mainsheets for this reason. On the vang and downhaul, I make do with the tension achieved by hand. Do not use cam cleats on any line that will be heavily loaded.

Line Stoppers

Special line stoppers are now available for particular applications. Most are designed to be mounted on deck or mast. Some can be lined up in series. A problem with multiple stoppers is that it is usually impossible to achieve a true lead to the winch in both horizontal and vertical planes for all of the lines. Vertical stacking of stoppers solves the lateral lead problems but creates problems of lines slipping off the winch if they lead from below or of riding turns if they bear from above.

Side-by-side mounting creates other problems. Considerable chafe occurs on one of CYCLURA's side-by-side mounted stoppers for the mainsheet and main halyard. I considered this problem carefully when I did the installation, and, given the design, there was no reasonable way to get both lines to lead without some chafe. A stopper with a sheave or roller on either side of the exit end would solve this problem nicely and allow the rope to bear laterally in any direction with a 90° sector or more.

Line stoppers are also available mounted in turning blocks for headsail sheets. Double-turning blocks with stoppers look like they should provide fair leads for two sheets to one winch. I have trouble imagining when this would function nearly as well as having separate winches for trimming each sheet — it would be disastrous for staysail and jib sheets on a cutter.

Stoppers are available with one of two types of release: either a hand-operated bar handle or a hole that accepts a winch handle. The latter type probably provides enough leverage to release under very heavy loads, which is not desirable.

Many of the shortcomings of cam cleats are largely overcome by line stoppers. The principle is much the same as the cam cleat but the single jaw has a larger bearing surface on the line, and the mechanism is actively disengaged by means of a hand lever. Line tension, through friction on the cam, pulls the cam forward and causes it to clamp down on the rope. If this load is substantial, the cam cannot be released until the line is pulled back through the stopper and the tension equalized, presumably with a winch.

Chocks

As with cleats, a critical consideration with chocks is the minimum radius that rope will contact. Some chocks have such sharp edges that rope cannot be left in them even briefly without anti-chafing gear, or damage will occur. Another shortcoming of many designs is that they are excessively directional — the rope lead is fair and non-chafing for about 60°, but beyond this sector, chafe occurs. Size is also important, as with cleats; and all other things being equal, a larger chock will almost always be an improvement.

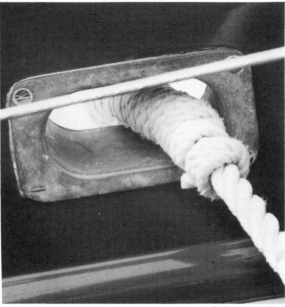

A hawse pipe.

The classic skein-type chock is a good design; it is unfortunate that it has often been replaced by less successful, more recent designs. Closed chocks are slightly harder to use because the line end must be threaded through, but this is a small cost to pay in exchange for the certainty that the rope will not pop out. Very neat closed chocks can be added to stainless steel bow fittings by welding on heavy bar stock bent into the appropriate shape.

I am especially partial to an old-fashioned chock design which incorporates two rollers, one on either side of the rope. These lead fair over a 180° sector and minimize chafe. Those I have seen were intricate bronze castings, which could be copied without too much trouble. It would also be fairly easy to make them up from stainless steel.

Yachts with bulwarks can fit hawse pipes, which are a very neat system. In fact, hawse pipes justify the bulwarks, at least forward, on large yachts, 50 feet and over.

A cockpit winch.

A halyard winch.

Fairleads

I have yet to see a bad fairlead design, but I have seen many poor installations. Fairleads should be used only to keep a line or cable in the same position — taut or slack. Lines should never be turned by fairleads. On spars, fairleads are useful to prevent slack lines from fouling on other gear. On deck, they can be used to smooth the path over a potential chafe point, and on small boats they are often used to lead lines through the deck.

Winches

A comprehensive consumer's guide to winches would be welcomed by many sailors, but I am unable to embark on such an extensive project here. My overall impression is that quality and price are closely correlated in comparable winches from different manufacturers. One possible consideration in selecting one brand over another is that brand-name winches add to the resale value of a

yacht out of proportion to their higher cost.

Winches are advertised by their gear ratios; or, often by so-called "power ratios," which is a fancy term for mechanical advantage. One should probably think in terms of working loads when selecting winches: the mechanical advantage multiplied by the human force to be applied, which is usually about 50 pounds. The optimum winch for any application is one that can load the line to its working load (but not far beyond) without excessive exertion on the part of the operator.

Winches are available with bronze, chromed bronze, stainless steel, anodized aluminum or titanium drums. Anodized aluminum is the least expensive and is completely satisfactory for most uses. Its only drawback is that wire cable will damage it. Some hot-shot racers simply replace the drums when the damage is severe. The cruiser's solution is to measure halyards so that only the tail is winched, never the wire. With proper tail splices, this causes no problems.

Blocks

Very inexpensive blocks tend to be very poor indeed. Several years ago, I installed an awning on the porch of my house and used some galvanized blocks in the roll-up mechanism. After a few months, the sheaves stopped turning, and the work involved in raising the awning increased enormously. Good blocks are a good investment.

Advertising literature for some blocks mentions nothing about strength; such blocks should be shunned. Some advertise a breaking strength, and others a working load. It is hard to know what to make of the notion of breaking strength in the case of blocks, because a block may become seriously deformed or totally disabled long before it actually falls apart. My estimate, derived from comparing designs and prices, is that a safe or reasonable working load may be arrived at by dividing advertised breaking strengths roughly by four. Working load specs, presumably, can be taken at face value.

The lead through blocks often causes problems. When under tension, the plane formed by the entering and exiting parts of the rope should always be perpendicular to the sheave axis. If the sheave and the rope do not lie in the same plane, a bending stress is being applied to the head of the block, causing wear to both block and rope. Two situations where this occurs are in deck blocks which reach the limit of their swivel range, and in snatch blocks attached to slotted toe rails with shackles too small to move and align freely. In both cases, different types of blocks are required. The deck block can be replaced with a properly aligned turning block and a trunnion shackle added to the snatch block. The same problem arises with the installation of turning blocks. As such

154

blocks are fixed, their alignment must be very carefully set.

Blocks should be periodically examined to see if any cracks have developed that might

snag rope fibers or be serious enough to weaken the structure. In the case of minor cracks, sanding with emery paper may be an adequate solution. Blocks with serious defects should be returned to the manufacturer or retailer rather than discarded.

Turnbuckles

Turnbuckles now do the job that used to be done by deadeyes and lanyards in the old days. There are still some boats in use that use the old gear, and they are pleasing to the eye; but turnbuckles definitely constitute a giant step forward as a means of regulating the length, and hence the tension, of standing rigging.

The traditional turnbuckle design relies on cotter pins to lock the screws when the device is not being adjusted, and this constitutes my main complaint about turnbuckles. The pins create a serious chafe problem and often a hazard of personal injury. Many generations of designs have failed to solve this problem, but fortunately designers are now beginning to address themselves to its solution. Some of the newer designs use nut locking systems — a big improvement. Others have closed bodies with a narrow slit accommodating a patent locking pin or wire. These seem to work quite well.

Turnbuckle size numbers refer to the thread sizes. This diameter should be between ⅛ and ¼ inch greater than the diameter of the standing rigging, because the fitting should be at least as strong as the wire — the perishable item in the system — and the threads weaken the metal. The toggles on American turnbuckles use clevis pins of the same diameter as the screws, whereas the British use smaller pins. The American system has the virtue of being easier to

remember, although the extra strength is not needed because the clevis pin is unthreaded and in shear. All of the best turnbuckles are made of stainless steel, and have proven to be satisfactory in terms of corrosion and galling.

Tackles

The only tackles regularly found on contemporary sailboats are mainsheet tackles and boom vangs.

Most modern sailors have a limited idea of the versatility of tackles. Almost invariably, when I am serving a splice stretched out with a tackle, getting my dinghy on deck with a tackle, raising a deck-stepped mast with a tackle, or using a tackle for anything but a mainsheet or vang, someone comments on my originality and inventiveness.

Winches have largely replaced tackles as the normal means of applying mechanical advantage in handling lines on sailboats. On power boats under 40 feet there is not likely to be any such device on board. Sportfishermen usually have a tackle for getting the "big one" on board and some power boats have dinghy davits. Most larger power yachts have windlasses, but usually have no blocks.

One story suffices to demonstrate the versatility of tackles on all boats. Ellen was airing the bunk cushions on IPHISA'S deck, when a gust blew one into the water. I dove in and caught up with it about 100 feet away. I easily swam back with the cushion in tow, but noticed that it was getting waterlogged. The two of us could not get it aboard. I put a line around it and hoisted it aboard with the mainsheets. Without a tackle, the cushion (or an unconscious person) would have been lost. Every boat bigger than a daysailer should carry one good tackle — a four-part tackle rove with ½-inch line is a good size.

155

Sheaves

A double-sheave exit box.

Metal sheaves are required only for wire cable. Plastic sheaves from reputable manufacturers appear to be very durable. I know of only a few cases of failure; they were speedily adjusted by the company.

There is no advantage to using sheaves wider than the diameter of the rope running through them; in the case of very inelastic materials such as Kevlar and wire, there is a definite disadvantage to flattening the structure in a broad sheave. This is why wire halyards with rope tails are run in special sheaves that have a narrow groove within a wider groove.

Internal halyards present some special problems that the yachtsman should be aware of. The halyard or lift can get in and

out of the spar in two different ways. It can either take an abrupt turn around a sheave mounted in the spar wall or it can make its abrupt turns outside of the spar, making only minor changes of direction when traversing the wall. The former approach should probably only be used at the masthead, where a strong and complex fitting can be fabricated to ensure that all leads are fair. If a halyard comes out of the mast below the top and in so doing makes a sharp turn, a large sheave will be mounted in a fitting set in a big slot cut in the extrusion and held by screws to the wall. This kind of attachment is unsatisfactory because the sheave tends to be inaccessible and because the substantial downward load is inadequately opposed by the screws in the spar wall.

Except at the masthead, it is better to get the halyards in and out of the spar with double sheave boxes, and then to redirect them with properly mounted blocks outside. In the case of a staysail, for example, a large block should be hung from the inner forestay tang and the halyard should emerge from the mast at least a foot below. At the base of the mast, it is best to get the halyards out eight or nine feet above the deck so that they can be pulled by hand by someone standing at the mast. If winches are not mast-mounted, which is probably best, blocks can be mounted around the mast, either on the deck or on a strong deck-mounted ring, to lead to winches. This solves two persistent problems with a deck-level exit box — getting the sheaves to point in the right direction and getting them at the right level above the deck.

Yachtsmen tend to think of sheaves only as components of made-up fittings and to ignore the numerous possibilities of mounting sheaves in fittings custom-fabricated to suit a particular need. Loose sheaves are

156

available and are easily mounted between two stainless steel plates or in a casting. All that most sheaves require is clearance and a pin or bar to function as axle.

Shackles

As I have bent and broken quite a few shackles over the years, I now buy them by the dozen from reputable manufacturers who advertise strengths. I keep the number of types of shackles aboard to a minimum and I keep plenty of spares of each type on hand at all times. I carry snap shackles for the tack and halyard of headsails; two sizes of stainless steel bow shackles for general purposes, including the main halyard; and one size of galvanized shackle for chains and anchors. This simple system works much better than the usual situation, which is to have a great range of sizes and shapes, each of which will do only one particular job. The single flaw in my system is the main tack — I am now more or less convinced that no shackle is made that will fit it. My solution has been to bend one of my standard shackles very much out of shape, drill out its threads, and run a bolt through it, which is not quite Bristol fashion.

Lifeline Fittings

A great many sailors fail to take lifelines seriously. It seems to me that as a potential last link with the corporeal world in stormy seas, they deserve serious consideration indeed. Most fittings for lifelines are lightweight and of unknown strength. They do not meet my criteria. Use fittings — turnbuckles, pelican hooks, terminals, and shackles — designed for standing rigging, and your lifelines will pass my test. If you can stand on them, you can rely on them.

Mounting Hardware

The attachment of deck and spar hardware is often very inadequate. Probably the most inadequately installed items are stanchions and pulpits, but winches, tracks, cleats, and almost anything else mentioned in this chapter have been known to work loose, either gradually or suddenly.

Two factors must be taken into consideration to properly mount any piece of hardware: the maximum force that is likely to be applied to the hardware, and the strength of the point of attachment.

Winches require that their load be spread over an area wider than the winch base. This is done be securing the winch on a mount which is about twice as wide as the winch base and which has eight or more screw holes. Such mounts are available as standard items scaled to various winch sizes. Tangs also require that their load be distributed over as wide an area as possible; one should choose the largest that can be accommodated on the spar to be used.

Extruded spars vary both in external dimensions and in wall thickness. Greater external size increases stiffness, while greater wall thickness provides stronger screw mounting. Any aluminum spar should be strong enough to support cleats attached with two machine screws run into tapped holes. Some extrusions have such thin walls that pop rivets must be used instead of screws. These are not recommended.

Some boom bails are attached by a single through-bolt, on which the bail pivots. Unless a through-tube is welded in for the bolt to bear on, the holes will elongate, eventually destroying the boom. Bails which are attached by several machine screws are a sounder installation.

Virtually no deck is strong enough by itself to properly hold a windlass, mid-deck mooring cleat, or Samson post, with simple through-bolting. Samson posts should be mounted through to the stem and heavily supported at the deck with partners. A large mid-deck cleat requires at least a substantial backing plate. If the deck is lightweight, an athwartship partner and a vertical tie rod may be in order. Windlasses require a partner for their aft bolts on even the strongest decks. On light decks, two partners with a tie rod through the aft one provide a sound installation.

Very lightweight decks, such as those cored with airex or balsa, will collapse under the compression of through-bolts. It is essential with such decks to replace the light core material with plywood or solid fiberglass wherever fittings are to be mounted. Other decks can withstand this compression as long as it is not concentrated on a very small area, such as that provided by a conventional washer. Backing plates distribute such loads effectively and should be used on absolutely all deck fastenings. These can be quickly made from stainless steel bar stock for concealed parts of the overhead. In the middle of the cabin, bronze castings, ¼-inch thick and of appropriate shape, are more attractive. These castings are drilled and tapped for screws, which should never be less than a ½ inch from the edge of the casting. For single screws, a button 1½ inches in diameter works well. A ring shape works well for winches. To finish off such installations, the screw ends are filed flush and the overhead, plates and all, is painted over.

Mainsheet tracks are occasionally subjected to very heavy loads, such as those resulting from an accidental jibe. The backing plate for the mainsheet track can be a long stainless steel bar which extends to the hull-deck join, where it can be bolted with the toe-rail bolts. If there is any question of the deck being strong enough to oppose the upward forces on the mainsheet track, tie rods can be used to connect the backing plate to the hull.

Fabrication of Hardware

Most yachtsmen, including some who have done extensive boat carpentry or glass work, are not aware that custom fittings are relatively easy to make. Provided one does most of the work oneself, they are also relatively inexpensive. There is little need to bemoan the lack of some item in a particular size or configuration in the catalogues — you can make it yourself. The two metals that suit most such work are welded stainless steel and cast bronze. Stainless steel is preferred where strong, thin structures, perhaps braced in various directions, are desired. Examples are stem fittings with anchor rollers, chain-plates and other attachment points, and bridges on which to mount mainsheet tracks. Bronze is used for structures which are bulkier and which need not oppose very concentrated stress; rudder heads and backing plates are best made from bronze. Tiller straps can be made from either bronze or stainless steel. The latter results in a lighter structure but requires a great deal of hacksaw work, while the former is heavier, easier to make, and prettier to look at.

Stainless steel is fashioned into fittings by cutting pieces from bar, angle, or rod stock and then having them welded together by a professional, according to your design. The cost of welding is usually considerably less than the cost of the metal; the amount saved by doing your own design, cutting, and fitting is at least five times the cost of materials and welding combined.

The first step is to develop a general design. If the fitting must fit a particular shape, such as a bow, a tracing of that shape is the starting point. Do not worry about what pieces will make up the structure at this point; just sketch the ideal configuration. Measure carefully all pieces that must fit into the structure being designed. Will the anchors fit into the rollers, will the bridge fit over the cabin, will the track fit over the bridge, etc.? Now decide what shapes cut from stock will fit together to make the whole. Take the sketches to your welder and ask for guidance. He may well recommend alterations that will facilitate both his job and yours. If very heavy stock is to be used, it is efficient to have it cut on a power saw. Some filing may be required to make bevels that will take the weld. If the piece is made up of many parts, it is best to weld them together two or three at a time, and then cut the next parts to fit in place. Drilling stainless steel requires a drill press and cutting oil, but the charge will be less if you lay out the location to be drilled before you take the piece to a machine shop. If you are careful, the results will be satisfactory and much less expensive than custom fabrication by a professional and maybe even less than stock items.

Bronze casting is done by pressing a dummy pattern into special sand to make a mold into which molten bronze is poured. Casting is done at a foundry and the charge is based on the amount of metal used. You make the patterns. In making a pattern, one must always keep in mind that it has to be pressed into sand and then pulled out. Flared shapes, which will damage the shape of the sand as they are extracted, are not possible.

The solution, if such shapes are required, is to eliminate the flare by making the pattern larger than the finished piece and then to grind off the excess metal after casting.

Most patterns are easily made of wood. Backing plates can be cut from ¼-inch plywood and then the edges rounded with a shaper, router, or rasp. Other, larger patterns can be fashioned from soft pine, balsa, or other easily worked wood. To achieve a fine finish on the bronze, the wood should be carefully sanded, which in some cases may require filling and sealing. If many small pieces such as backing plates are to be cast, they can be glued to a board and pressed into the sand at one time.

After casting, bronze can be drilled, sawed, filed, and machined in other ways. Drill points can be indicated on the pattern by small depressions, which will come out as useful drilling points. The easiest treatment of bronze is to paint it over, as with backing plates on the cabin overhead. It can also be polished and chrome-plated. Be sure that the plating is a proper marine job with a nickel base and heavy chrome.

Many yacht-building yards keep a supply of patterns they have made and used over the years. For a small charge, or perhaps gratis, they will let you take a casting from these patterns. New England Boatbuilders in Mattapoisett have many of L. Francis Herreshoff's patterns, which are a veritable trove, and I am sure there are many other such collections to be found. Even an existing piece of hardware can serve as a pattern for a duplicate. In this way, classic designs can be reproduced and used.

Chapter 8
Forces and loads

Yachtsmen design their own assemblies of rope, chain, and associated hardware more often than not. The base of knowledge drawn from in this design process is usually tradition or conventional wisdom. Even professional riggers rely heavily on traditional knowledge; only a very few are trained engineers or metallurgists.

In the world of boating, not only finanical considerations, but, ultimately, the lives and safety of the crew depend on the absolute reliability of each component of the system. It therefore behooves the yachtsman to be knowledgeable about the capacities of the materials he relies on and the magnitude of the demands he makes on them, whether or not he actually does his own rigging.

Relatively few yachtsmen, I think, clearly understand the relationship between the published strength statistics for the ropes and cables they buy and the sizes of loads those ropes and cables should actually be bearing in normal use. Nor, in all likelihood, do many have a clear understanding of the magnitudes of the loads and forces they are dealing with; nor the ways in which, or the circumstances under which those loads can get out of hand, exceeding the capacities of the rigging materials to bear them.

In many yachting applications, very generous safety factors are used as a matter of custom, so that failures of most types of cordage (anchor rodes or jib sheets, for example) are comparatively rare. When failure does occur, it surprises the traditionalist, who blames the mishap on some invisible weakness in his materials. The materials are seldom at fault, however, and many failures could be foreseen and prevented if elementary engineering knowledge were brought to bear.

Failures are more frequent in the area of standing rigging. Rigs on racy boats are often designed very lightly for maximum speed. If the yachtsman, unaware of the limitations of his equipment, pushes it beyond its limits — as he can easily do — the consequences can be both disastrous and expensive.

Tradition and conventional wisdom represent a cross section of accumulated empirical experience. They constitute a valuable body of knowledge that goes a long way toward supplying the yachtsman with the information he needs. I suggest, however, that a little elementary applied physics and engineering can be of more practical use.

Yachtsmen deal regularly with highly technical matters — navigation, for example — and I have the impression that, as a breed, they have something of a penchant for the technical. Perhaps the average yachtsman does not have the technical knowledge required to deal numerically with the problem of designing a rigging assembly because no discussion of the elementary engineering that bears on these matters has been readily available. This information is simple enough that no one need be scared off.

Forces

In selecting and using cordage we are ultimately dealing with the problem of harnessing and transferring physical stresses and loads, or, more simply, **forces**. The physicist's definition of force is that which accelerates or decelerates matter. The size or magnitude of a force is measured by both the **mass** of the object (the amount of matter accelerated) and the amount of acceleration that occurs. The equation relating these three variables is:

$$F = m \times a; \text{ or}$$
$$\text{Force} = \text{mass times acceleration.}$$

Mass, again by a physicist's definition, is the resistance of an object to changes in its state of motion; another word for this is inertia. Ultimately, the only way to measure mass is in terms of how hard you have to push (how much force you must exert) to get it moving or to stop it. In a sense, then, mass and force are defined in terms of one another.

Acceleration and Gravity

Acceleration and **deceleration** are *changes* in the *rate* of motion of an object, and such a change in rate of motion will take place only so long as a force is being applied to the object in question. Once an object has been set in motion (accelerated to a certain velocity) it will continue to travel at that rate without any force being applied. (This, again, is a manifestation of its mass or inertia.)

All objects on earth are subject to an acceleration imposed by the earth's gravitational field. In free fall near the earth's surface, objects all accelerate at the same rate — 32 feet per second per second (32 ft/sec^2) — which means that during each second of fall, the object's rate of speed increases by a factor of 32 feet per second. Starting from a point of rest, at the end of one second, a free-falling object will be traveling at a velocity of 32 feet per second. At the end of two seconds of fall, it will be traveling at a velocity of 64 feet per second, and so on.

Weight and Force

Weight, which many of us think of as being identical to mass, is actually a special kind of force: the force exerted by an object due to the fact that its mass is being accelerated by gravity. If I stand on a scale, it tells me that gravity is accelerating my mass with a force of about 165 pounds. What, then, is the measure of my mass? To clear up this question we must understand one of the significant ambiguities of our language. Both mass and force are measured in units called pounds — we could call them "mass pounds" and "force pounds." A pound of mass is a measure of a concrete amount of matter having a constant inertia. What, then, is a pound of force? It is the force *equivalent* to that exerted by one pound of mass subject to the acceleration of gravity or *its* equivalent. By pulling on the end of a rope with my one manpower, I am generating a force *equivalent* to that of 50 pounds of mass being accelerated by gravity. All measurements of force expressed in pounds are relating mass to a specific or constant rate of acceleration: 32 ft/sec^2. To put it yet another way, every time we say "*x* pounds of force," we are in effect saying "*x* pounds of mass times *g*" (*g* being the conventional symbol for gravitational acceleration).

Let us consider some simple examples that should help to clarify these relationships.

EXAMPLE I. If a person standing on a dock pulls on the bow line of a 10-ton (20,000-pound) yacht with a force of 50 pounds (one manpower), we can easily calculate the acceleration that will result. (Although it may seem unnecessarily tedious, it is a good idea at this stage to avoid leaving out any steps in the logic — to make explicit as many of the factors in the calculation as possible.)

Starting with our formula $F = m \times a$, we first rearrange the equation to solve for acceleration: $a = \dfrac{F}{m}$. Next, we "plug in" our known values and the equation is written $a = \dfrac{50 \text{ "mass pounds"} \times g}{20,000 \text{ "mass pounds"}}$. Dividing, we get $a = .0025 \times g$. We know that g is 32 ft/sec^2; thus, $a = .0025 \times 32$ ft/sec^2 or .08 ft/sec^2.

EXAMPLE II. The question of the force necessary to stop a massive yacht is often of much greater practical concern than that of how to get it moving. This is certainly true in docking situations. If our 10-ton yacht is moving past a dock at a velocity of 8 feet per second (about 4.7 knots), and a stern line is thrown to a person on the dock who passes it around a piling and commences to exert a 50-pound force in opposition to the boat's motion, we can calculate how long it will take to bring the boat to a halt.

The same formula ($F = m \times a$) applies equally to acceleration and deceleration. We know from our first example that a 50-pound force exerted on a 20,000-pound mass results in an acceleration or deceleration of .08 ft/sec². The initial speed of the boat is 8 ft/sec and the deceleration is .08 ft/sec², so in each second, the 50-pound force will decrease that initial speed by 1/100 part — by a factor of .08 ft/sec — and the boat will come to a stop in 100 seconds. As the average velocity during this time was 4 ft/sec, the boat will have traveled 400 feet in coming to a halt. The same 50-pound force would take only 10 seconds to stop a 10-ton boat with a velocity of .8 ft/sec, and this would be accomplished in a distance of only 4 feet. If more helmsmen understood this, boats would come into docks much more slowly than they usually do and there would be considerably less grunting and groaning, and much less damage.

EXAMPLE III. Suppose a 10-ton boat is coming directly toward a dock at a speed of one knot and has to be stopped by its stern line to a piling or an anchor before it travels another 10 feet in order avoid crashing into the dock. We know the initial velocity of the boat — one knot — which equals 1.7 ft/sec, and the distance — 10 feet — in which the deceleration has

to take place. From these we can calculate both the rate of deceleration and the force or load on the rope.

First, we need to know how long the deceleration will take. The average velocity in going from an initial velocity of 1.7 ft/sec to 0 is one-half of the initial velocity or .85 ft/sec. Covering 10 feet at an average speed of .85 ft/sec will take 11.7 seconds. The rate of deceleration is found by dividing the initial velocity by the time of the deceleration $a = \frac{iv}{t}$. Thus, $a = \frac{1.7 \text{ ft/sec}}{11.7 \text{ sec}}$ and we find that the rate of deceleration is .145 ft/sec².

To find the force in pounds (the load acting on the rope), we must convert our numbers into terms of an acceleration (in this case, deceleration) equivalent to that of gravity — .145 ft/sec² is 1/220th of g (or .0045 × 32 ft/sec²); 1/220th of the mass of the boat (or .0045 × 20,000 pounds) is 91 pounds. The force decelerating 20,000 pounds at the rate of .145 ft/sec² is *equivalent* to the force decelerating 91 pounds at the rate of 32 ft/sec². The load on the rope is 91 pounds of force, which can be easily absorbed by a typical ½-inch nylon dock line.

Work and Power

When a sailor stands holding a sheet or other rope under tension, no work, strictly speaking, is being performed. This may seem contradictory as he will probably get tired, but the same end could be achieved by belaying the line on a cleat, and we certainly don't think of the cleat as performing work. **Work** involves the application of a force to *move* something, as in pulling in a sheet. In figure A₁ we see a weight of 10 pounds exerting a downward force that is opposed by an equal and opposite tension in a rope. In figure A_2 the 10-pound weight has been lifted one foot. In the first case, force is being exerted but no work has taken place; whereas in the second the weight has been moved, and we say that work has been done. The amount of work done is expressed as 10 **foot-pounds** (10 ft-lbs). It is equal to the amount of work involved in moving five pounds up two feet or to that of moving 20 pounds up one-half foot (figure A_3) — all, of, course, against the force of gravity. We can write a simple equation for work:

$$W = f \times s; \text{ or}$$
$$\text{Work} = \text{force times distance}$$

(s is the conventional symbol for distance).

Power is the capacity to do work, and its measurement depends on how rapidly the work is done. If the 10-pound weight in figure A_2 is lifted one foot in one second, the power involved is 10 **foot-pounds per second**, (10 ft-lbs/sec). If the weight is lifted five feet in one second or one foot in 1/5 of a second, the power is 50 ft-lbs/sec, which is approximately one manpower. One horsepower, which is the other unit of power in common usage, equals 550 ft-lbs/sec, or roughly 11 manpower.

Mechanical Advantage

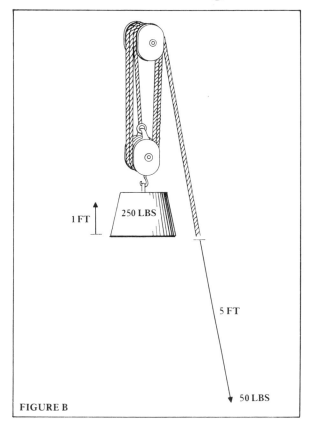

FIGURE B

Simple mechanical devices (such as levers, tackles, gears, etc.) can be used to vary the *ratio* between force and distance in the application of power to do work. This is called utilizing a **mechanical advantage**. The amount of *work* performed does not change, but the amount of *force* applied is multiplied to the same extent that the *distance* is divided. Consider the case of a five-part tackle (see figure B). If you pull in five feet on the fall (free end) with a force of 50 pounds, that work (250 ft-lbs) will be transferred to the movable block as a force of 250 pounds moving one foot. The tackle is said to have a 5-to-1 mechanical advantage.

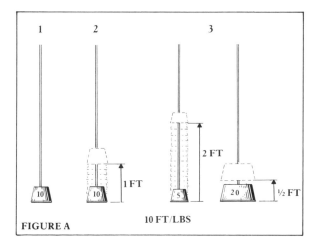

FIGURE A

10 FT/LBS

165

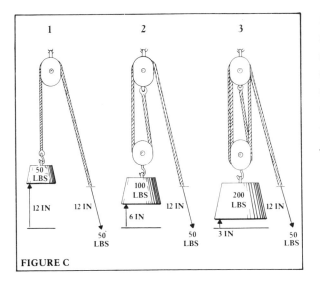

FIGURE C

500 pounds, and the rode comes in at one foot in 10 seconds. The amount of power applied to do work and the amount of work done by one man remain constant — a man cannot greatly exceed 50 ft-lbs/sec regardless of what mechanical device he operates — but as the example illustrates, the amount of *force* he can bring to bear can be multiplied, and this can make the difference between getting the job done and not.

Static and Dynamic Loads

In analyzing the loads placed on ropes, etc., we need to distinguish clearly between **static loads,** in which a balance or equilibrium exists between the load and the structure resisting it and in which no apparent acceleration or deceleration is taking place, and **dynamic loads,** in which the acceleration or deceleration *is* apparent. An object suspended on a line, for example, exerts a static load on that line (due to the acceleration of earth's gravitation). On the other hand, when a motorboat takes off with a skier in tow, the tow rope becomes taut and is dynamically loaded as the boat and skier accelerate to hull speed. Once hull speed is reached, assuming the skier makes no maneuvers that place lateral stresses on the rope, it relaxes somewhat but remains statically loaded with the weight of the skier plus the force of the drag of friction between the skis and the water.

The significance of dynamic loading becomes most apparent in situations where ropes, etc., are called upon to accelerate or decelerate very massive or rapidly moving objects in relatively short distances or time spans. Forces can be multiplied by factors of several hundred or more, depending on the situation and the properties of the materials in question. Let us consider some examples.

The mechanical advantage of a tackle depends on the number of "parts" — the number of lines among which the load is distributed. In figure C, 1 is a "one-part tackle," so to speak, and has no mechanical advantage; 2 is a two-part tackle and has a 2-to-1 advantage; 3 is a four-part tackle and has a 4-to-1 mechanical advantage. (Note: if the fall leads from the moving block, it constitutes a "part" of the tackle.)

For another simple mechanical advantage example involving the lever principle, see the section on single-action winches, Chapter 5.

Manpower is used for many purposes on a boat, and it is quite useful to know what manpower can and cannot do. For example, an anchor rode may be under 50 pounds of tension as it is being hauled in by hand. One man should be able to haul the rode in at approximately one foot per second. If the rode is under 500 pounds of tension, a man cannot possibly haul it in by hand. But a man operating a mechanical windlass with a 10-to-1 mechanical advantage can pull in a rode under 500 pounds of tension. The one manpower is applied to the rode as a force of

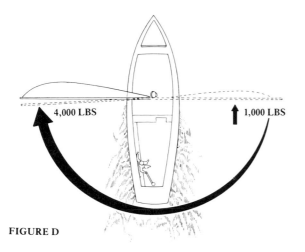

FIGURE D

EXAMPLE I. I have calculated that the load on CYCLURA's mainsail, running before the wind at hull speed, is about 1,000 pounds. The load on the mainsheet and mainsheet tackle that would result from an accidental jibe would be a combination of the static load generated by the wind on the sail and the dynamic load resulting from the acceleration of the mass of the boom as it goes from one tack to the other. The boom is about 20 feet long and has a mass of about 100 pounds. If the boom swings 180° in two seconds, its center of mass, 10 feet from the gooseneck, will reach a maximum velocity of about 30 ft/sec. If the sheets stop this boom in six inches, the deceleration will be at an average velocity of 15 ft/sec, covering six inches in 1/30 sec, or 900 ft/sec², which is almost 30 times gravity. Thirty g's acting on the boom's 100-pound mass will generate a force of 3,000 pounds. Adding this dynamic load to the static load gives a total of 4,000 pounds — uncomfortably close to the breaking strength of the gear (see figure D). This kind of accident often pulls the fittings out or breaks shackles. The greater danger in a jibe, however, is the boom hitting the backstay. The lateral load is usually great enough to break the stay and bring down the whole rig.

EXAMPLE II. A 150-pound man is working on a bosun's chair 55 feet above deck. He is supported by a 7 x 19 stainless steel cable halyard led to a reel winch and he has not attached his safety line. The winch brake releases suddenly, as they occasionally do, and he free-falls for about a second. The brake is now abruptly applied by the panicked deck man, and the rigger in the bosun's chair quickly loses his velocity towards the deck. The halyard is about 80 feet long and will stretch about one inch. Velocity after one second is 32 ft/sec so that the deceleration is from that speed to zero in the time it takes to travel one inch. The average speed over this inch will be about 16 ft/sec, and the inch will be covered in about .005 (1/200) second. The deceleration is now 32 feet per second per .005 second, which calculates out to 6,400 ft/sec² (200 × 32 ft/sec²) or 200 times gravity. Thus, the load on the halyard will be 200 times the man's 150-pound weight — 30,000 pounds. The halyard would undoubtedly break, and the man would probably die from such rapid deceleration.

If in the same situation the halyard were of nylon, the bosun would fare much better. If the halyard stretches 16 feet in decelerating his mass — perfectly possible with nylon rope — the deceleration will occur over a full second. The dynamic load is thus 32 ft/sec², which is the equivalent of the static load due to gravity. Thus, the combined load on the rope is twice the man's weight, or 300 pounds, which is perfectly safe with ½-inch nylon line.

Scalars and Vectors

Quantitative measurements in science and engineering fall into two distinct categories. The simpler kind, called **scalar quantities** or

just **scalars,** have magnitude only. They are adequately described in terms of a number of units of some measurement scale, such as degrees (temperature), feet (distance), or minutes (time).

The other kind, **vector quantities** or **vectors,** have both magnitude and direction and thus require two pieces of descriptive information for complete expression.

Velocities, for example, are vector quantities that yachtsmen deal with all the time. The speed of a current and of a boat through the water are essential but insufficient data to determine where that boat will end up after a given time. To solve that problem we also need to know the direction of the current and the boat's course-direction and starting point.

Forces and accelerations are the vector quantities with which we will be dealing most extensively in the coming pages.

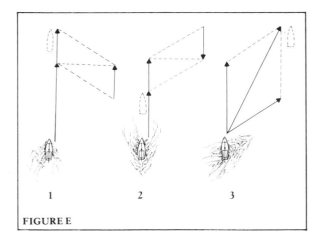

FIGURE E

The arithmetic for vectors is different from that for scalars in order to take the point of application and direction into account. Once it is understood, which is not difficult, this arithmetic makes as much intuitive sense as scalar arithmetic. Let us consider various possibilities of the boat-and-current velocity

problem as an example. If current and boat are moving in the same direction (figure E_1), the velocities are simply added; the boat reaches its destination sooner than it would if there were no current. If the current is running in the opposite direction to the boat's velocity (figure E_2), then the current velocity must be subtracted; the boat takes longer to reach its destination. But what happens if the current velocity and the boat velocity form an angle other than 0° or 180° as in these two simple cases? Both the direction and the rate of travel change when the two velocities are added. The addition can be done diagrammatically by construction of a parallelogram, as shown in figure E_3.

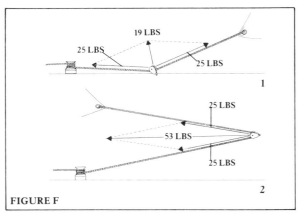

FIGURE F

Let us consider a simple vector addition problem dealing with forces. Suppose that a jibsheet is being led through a deck block to the winch used to haul in on the line in sheeting. If a force of 25 pounds is being exerted on each part of the line, what is the force being exerted on the block and its mounting? The answer depends on the lead angles that the lines assume (see figures F_1 and F_2). As you can see from the figures, the smaller the angle, the greater the load, and vice versa.

Load Angles

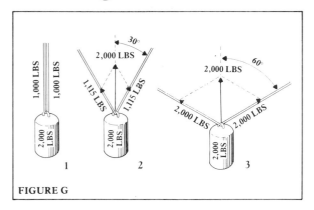

FIGURE G

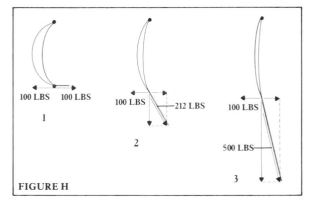

FIGURE H

One important application of vector addition to marlinspike practice is in the calculation of loads on ropes (or other tensile structures) which oppose force other than in a directly opposite direction. The bigger the angle, the greater the increase in load. (This is because part of the load opposes the force, and the rest opposes whatever prevents the force and the rope from assuming directions opposite to each other.) This phenomenon is illustrated in various degrees in figure G. The 2,000-pound weight is supported by a rope which passes through an eye, so that each part of the rope supports half of the weight. With the parts together, as in G_1, the load on each is 1,000 pounds. As the rope parts are moved apart, the load on each increases. An approximate calculation of the load can be made by graphical vector addition as shown in figures G_2 and G_3.

At very large load angles, the tension or load becomes very much larger than the force it is opposing. As the load angle approaches 90°, the load approaches infinity. If the angle were 89° in our example, the load on each rope would be 57,299 pounds. A 2° deflection — an 88° load-to-force angle — would give a load of 28,654 pounds on each rope.

Let us look at another illustration of the load-angle problem as it relates to the sheeting of a jib (see figure H). Let us assume, for the sake of simplicity, that the force of the wind is at right angles to the fore-and-aft axis of the boat and that the wind is exerting a force of 100 pounds on the jib. If it were possible (which it is not, for several reasons) to sheet the sail with a line parallel to the wind direction, that line would bear a load equal and opposite to the force of the wind on the sail. (A moment's reflection will make it clear that this is only a theoretical possibility: since the flexible line becomes, in effect, part of the sail shape, it will always become the tangent to an arc that makes some angle to the wind-force vector.) As the angle between the wind-force direction and the sheet increases, the size of the load on the line increases. Two possible positions have been sketched as sample vector analyses (figures H_2 and H_3).

I call this phenomenon the lateral load effect and refer to it often, especially in the following chapters. Among other things, it is the reason that headstays sag under sail load. This application alone makes the effect worthy of sailors' attention and understanding.

Chapter 9
Materials: ropes, cables, chain, rod

In this chapter we will survey and examine the various kinds of cordage in common current usage aboard yachts, with an eye to better understanding their physical properties and, ultimately, their performance capabilities.

We can divide yacht cordage into four categories: fiber ropes (both twisted and braided); wire cables; metal rod; and chain. Each of these has special attributes that make it especially suitable for particular applications, and these are determined by the characteristics of the materials they are made from as well as the way in which they are structured. We will consider both aspects of the matter.

Of the physical properties we will consider in our evaluation of these materials, probably the most important is tensile strength — the resistance of the material to breaking when stretched lengthwise. Close behind in importance are elasticity and flexibility. The remaining physical properties we need to consider relate to resistance to deterioration due to corrosion, abrasion, fatigue, and heat; and the practical question of ease, security, and permanence of knotting, splicing, fastening, and joining. To simplify the language in the following general discussion, I use the term "rope" to stand for all the various forms of cordage; the principles apply equally to all.

Ancient Egyptian papyrus rope. The three-strand structure with twisted yarns and strands is similar to that used today, more than 3,000 years later. Photo by Jeremy McCabe, courtesy of Marlow Ropes.

172

Breaking Strength

If any performance statistic is available for rope that you buy, it is likely to be a standard for the size of the load at which that rope will fail or break. This is commonly referred to as its **tensile strength**, but a more correct term is **breaking strength**, as the number quantifies or defines the *limit* of tensile strength of the rope in question. On first consideration, the breaking strength figure may seem like the basic definitive piece of information about the performance of your rope, but it falls far short of telling the whole story. A bit of further investigation will reveal the reason for this.

Working Loads

One very widespread and dangerous misconception among sailors is the notion that the breaking strength actually represents a load you might consider putting on a rope. The fact is, permanent damage may be done to a new rope at loads considerably below its breaking strength — loads that will not actually cause a rope to part may still seriously weaken it. If ropes are to have a reasonably long life and are to be reliable, it is essential that actual loads never approach the breaking strength. The maximum load to which we actually expect to subject a rope is called the **working load** and may be a small fraction of the breaking strength. The ratio between the breaking strength and the working load is called the **safety factor** — a term to which we shall return frequently. But if a rope's breaking strength is not the factor determining the load we place on it, what is? The critical factor involved here is what is called the **elastic limit** of the material.

Elasticity

When a rope is subjected to tension, it undergoes a change in form and size — a deformation engineers call **structural elongation**; the lay term is stretch. Elasticity is the capacity of a material to recover from deformation or return to its original size and shape. When the limits of a material's elasticity are exceeded — when it is stretched past its limit — it will not return entirely to its original size and shape, but it will remain permanently longer, thinner, and weaker. The engineer's term for this phenomenon is "plastic elongation." Stress (tension) produces strain (deformation). Past a certain limit of strain, the material will not recover fully, but suffers permanent damage.

The elastic limit varies considerably for different kinds of materials and structures. Stainless steel cables can undergo plastic elongation at 20 to 40 percent of breaking strength. The figure given for most ropes is around 60 percent. Steel rod rigging does not reach its elastic limit until loaded to 80 percent of its breaking strength. Safety factors are properly calculated in relation to the elastic limits of the materials, the load at which potential damage occurs rather than in relation to breaking strength or load where outright failure can be expected. In any application on boats, it is critically important that loads approaching the elastic limit be avoided and that all lines, etc., which have suffered plastic elongation be replaced.

Fiber Ropes

A confusing array of rope constructions is available to today's yachtsman. All of the major manufacturers offer types which they claim to be the best available for each and every application on boats. It would be a huge task to judge and balance the costs and benefits of all the various alternatives on a case-by-case basis (and probably of dubious value). I can, however, offer a systematic examination of the various available types in some detail and analyze their characteristics and usefulness in specific applications.

Modern Fibers

Natural fiber ropes are virtually gone from yachting. The place of linen, hemp, and sisal has been taken by a variety of man-made fibers which simply make better, stronger, more reliable ropes. The new fibers all come from the large family of chemical compounds called "polymers" — the long, chain-like, interlocking molecular structures that make up most of our modern plastics. Four different fibers — nylon, polyester, polypropylene, and Kevlar — are used to make virtually all yachting ropes today; nylon and polyester probably account for 95 percent of the total.

Nylon

Nylon fibers are strong and elastic. Consequently, nylon rope has high tensile strength — the Cordage Institute minimum standard for breaking strength for 1-inch nylon rope is 22,600 pounds — and relatively high elasticity — it will elongate by about 25 percent before reaching its elastic limit. (Note, however, that when wet, nylon rope loses perhaps as much as 15 percent of its tensile strength.) This makes nylon the rope of choice in the many applications where dynamic loading is expected and where, consequently, an elastic rope is desirable — primarily in anchor and dock lines.

Nylon has excellent resistance to deterioration due to the effects of sunlight (a problem with many polymers). Its melting point is about 500° F. This is high enough so that the rope is not in danger of melting due to the friction generated in winching or other operations, but it does make possible the cutting and permanent fusing of strand ends by use of a "hot knife" — a great convenience in much knot and splice work. Finally, its resistance to chafe (damage from abrasion) under unloaded conditions is quite good. But special problems arise for nylon ropes due to the fact that they are so often used in situations where chafing occurs under considerable tension such as a dock line passing through a chock. Without some special chafe protection nylon ropes are susceptible to considerable damage in these circumstances. (See the sections on Deterioration and Chafing.)

Polyester

Polyester (which goes under the trade names Dacron, Terylene, and Fortrel) is almost as strong as nylon, and in contrast to nylon, loses little or no strength when wet. The most important thing about polyester rope is that its elasticity is less than half that of nylon. This combination of high tensile strength with low elasticity makes it ideal for applications in which one doesn't want a rope to stretch — mainly for halyards and sheets. Polyester rope has about the same melting point as nylon and has similar resistance to photochemical deterioration. Its wear qualities are even better than nylon.

Polypropylene

Polypropylene is a thermoplastic which melts at low temperatures (250-350° F.) and has a density about 10 percent lower than

water. The latter fact accounts for one of the few positive attributes of polypro rope — it is the only commonly available rope that floats. The former constitutes probably the most serious of its many defects: it melts and parts at temperatures commonly produced under powerful winching or severe chafe. A catalogue of its other shortcomings includes its relative weakness — it has only about one-third the tensile strength of dry nylon; its stiffness and slipperiness, which makes knotting and splicing considerably more difficult; and its great susceptibility to photochemical deterioration unless protected by special pigments or chemical ultraviolet inhibitors. It is relatively inexpensive, however, so there is a lot of it around, and it is suitable for various kinds of non-rigging uses, such as deck lashings, clotheslines, flag halyards, painters, and the like.

Kevlar

Kevlar is a recent development from the Du Pont Company that has caused quite a stir in yachting circles. It has very high tensile strength — about twice that of nylon — which on a weight basis makes it "as strong as steel" according to the advertisements. Its elasticity is much lower than that of polyester and similar to that of steel. This high tensile strength and low elasticity are desirable qualities in many running rigging applications, but there are some serious problems with Kevlar. It is very abrasive and very brittle; if bent sharply the fibers cut one another. Consequently, it can't be knotted, and unless carefully handled with special splices, very large sheaves, and general coddling, Kevlar rope tends to self-destruct. Even with special treatment, its life can be expected to be very much shorter than that of polyester running

rigging. I feel that this is a material of little interest to all but the most competitive and most experimental yachtsmen.

Twisted Rope Construction

Years ago, four- and five-strand twisted ropes were available. Many of the classic knot books show elaborate knots and splices that can be done with such cordage. Today, virtually all but three-strand ropes have disappeared. Ropes of more than three strands are a thing of the past and will not be dealt with here.

If we take a twisted rope apart, we can see that each of its strands is made up of a bundle of yarns twisted together. The yarns can be made up either of individual fibers twisted together, in which case the rope is called "three-phase," or of smaller yarns twisted together which are made up of individual fibers, in which case the rope is "four-phase."

The twisting in each stage or phase of the rope structure runs opposite to the twisting of the adjacent phases. Figure A should make this clear.

In practical terms, the difference to the yachtsman is the length of fiber segments exposed at the surface of the rope. The finer these fibers are and the longer their exposure on the surface, the more prone they are to snagging and pulling out. Virtually all nylon twisted ropes should be of four-phase construction, because nylon fibers are extremely fine and prone to snagging (as in ladies' hosiery). Dacron need not be four-phase below ¼-inch diameter, and three-phase polypropylene ropes resist snagging up to about 1-inch diameter.

Aside from the quality and suitability of fiber and the appropriate phasing structure, the only thing remaining to determine the quality of twisted rope is the manner in

FOUR-PHASE TWISTED ROPE

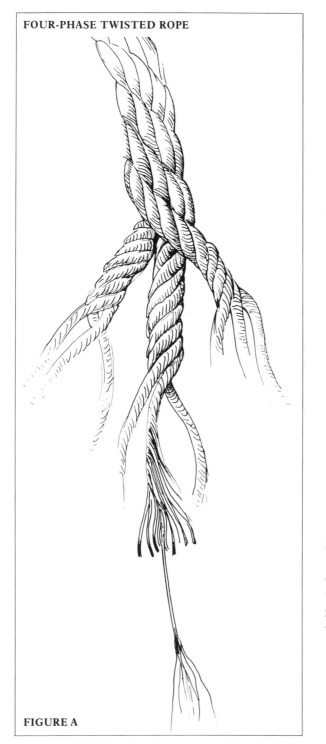

FIGURE A

which it is twisted. There are two aspects to twisting: how tightly the rope is layed up and how even the lays of the three or four independent twists are.

In practice, the only real difference between hard- and soft-lay ropes is in their elasticity. Contrary to most people's intuitive notions, hard ropes are more elastic than soft ones.

The question of evenness of loading is much more significant. Any seaman with substantial rope experience knows that some twisted ropes generate more torque under load than others. The best ropes produce no discernible torque; poor ropes can produce enough torque to untie knots or break out anchors.

Ropes and cables are structured so that all the components, be they wires, fibers, strands, or yarns, will be evenly loaded when the rope is under tension — the twists of rope, strands, and yarns opposing one another's torques. The torque that some ropes produce under tension is undoubtedly the result of an imbalance between rope and strand twists.

No test data have been published on this question to the best of my knowledge, but I do know that manufacturers are concerned about it as many own devices for precisely measuring the number of turns in a length of rope. One rope importer told me that one of the major problems with inexpensive imported rope is that it is not twisted enough and that some lots have to be rejected for this reason. Rope users should be very aware of this problem.

Braided Rope Construction

There are numerous types of braided ropes produced today, all of which would have been recognized in the forecastles of square-rigged whaling ships as "sennits." Each manufacturer, attempting to appear innovative, gives his ropes inventive trade names (and none calls them sennits). Abandoning an effort to list the commercial names, I have settled on using the classical terms as the simplest way to identify these simple patterns and avoid favoring one manufacturer over another by using his trade name. Today's solid-braid cord is identical to the crown sennit. In ropes of equal weight and fiber, solid-braid is only half as strong as hollow-braid since its construction involves nips such as occur in knots (see page 10). Solid-braid is inexpensive to manufacture and is widely used for utility purposes such as flag halyards, ties, and clotheslines, and especially as stock for decorative rope work; but it should not be used in any situation where strength is of any concern.

All the remaining braided ropes are of the square-sennit construction, which is tubular (hollow) in its geometry. In the United States, practically all available high-quality braid rope uses the tube-within-a-tube construction variously known as yacht braid, double-braid, braid-on-braid, or sheath-and-core. Eight-strand square sennit (usually with doubled strands) is the standard construction of both sheath and core for much double-braid. In sizes above ½ inch, however, 12-strand square sennit is sometimes used for the sheath; in small sizes, four-strand sennit is often used for the core.

British and European manufacturers produce a variety of braids not found here, many of which are single sennits of eight- to

Making yacht braid at the Cordage Group plant. A doubled 12-strand sheath is braided around the core.

178

twelve-strand construction with single, double, and occasionally quadruple strands. There is also a braid based on the four-strand sennit model, generally referred to as plaited rope. The most popular type, which is just beginning to be imported into this country and to be imitated by U.S. manufacturers is called, confusingly enough, "eight-plait" (due to the fact that each of the four strands is doubled).

Among the virtues of eight-plait is the fact that unlike any of the more complex braids, it can be successfully spliced like twisted rope by interweaving the strands.

There is one hermaphrodite rope construction that uses a three-strand twisted core and an eight-strand braided sheath. This completes the lineup of braided-rope types with which I am familiar.

Having gone through the process of cataloguing this great diversity of types, I must hasten to make the point that, advertising claims aside, there is no clear evidence that one type of hollow braid construction is generally superior to another. It is my belief that the diversity of construction types has the same origin as the diversity of names mentioned earlier — manufacturers trying to appear innovative, or at least different, in order to capture a piece of the market.

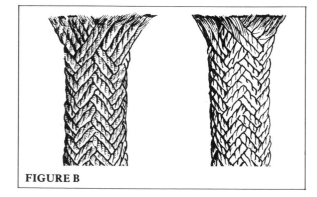

FIGURE B

Snagging

Fiber snagging is a matter of concern with braided as well as with twisted ropes, and there are differences in quality in this respect. One can, for example, buy ⅝-inch double braids in which the strands are simple twisted primary yarns. In terms of snag resistance, these compare poorly with other ⅝-inch double braids which have two-phase strands (see figure B). These differences are readily visible, and rope buyers should be alert to them.

Defects in Twisted Ropes

Aside from the question of proper phasing and adequate and proper twisting, most of the defects in twisted ropes have to do with the splicing of strand ends during manufacture. Strand splices, the places where the new material is joined in where the old spool ran out, are inherent weak spots in ropes. In the highest grades of rope there are no strand splices; the strand stock is longer than the finished rope. Considerable amounts of material are wasted to keep the quality high. Such rope is an expensive special-order item. For most of us, strand splices are a fact of life. However, I personally would return for exchange any spool of rope in which I could find two or more strand splices. One should not be able to find any without very careful inspection — they should be very carefully done.

The worst case I know of involved several hot-knife joins in a single anchor rode. These joins were so sloppily done that the rode snagged its own fibers. This rope was an "off-brand"; I hope that the major manufacturers would scrap rope of such low quality.

A second problem, which is especially

acute with nylon ropes, is that the rope is sometimes stretched onto the spool. This apparently occurs when rope is wound directly from the twisting machine, the spool supplying some of the tension needed to pull it through. The result is that considerable contraction can occur after the rope is purchased, even if it is measured as it is taken off the spool. It is commonly accepted that elastic products are purchased in relaxed lengths.

Defects in Braided Rope

As in twisted ropes, strand ends are the most annoying defect in braided ropes. My experience is that some manufacturers use much longer strands than others and consequently ends are much less frequent. I once found two ends within a few feet of each other while splicing braid onto 7x19 wire cable. Some rope makers tie strand ends together and bury the knot, which can remain hidden indefinitely. Such treatment only becomes evident when core and sheath are being separated for splicing — the knot can snag and pull some strands. A hot-knife join, which I have never seen in braided rope, would be disastrous in this regard. Some less expensive braided ropes have loose strand ends in the sheath, which eventually pull out.

Another defect I have observed in braided rope is core and sheath of unequal length. When I do a wire-to-rope splice, I milk the rope down to the free end. I once found that the core in a 50-foot length was some three feet longer than the sheath. This would presumably result in a considerable weakening of the rope, because only the core would come under tension. Occasionally a core will push through the sheath at a knot. This may also be a symptom of an overlength core.

Rope Selection — Twist versus Braid

In the United States, the choice of rope for a given application almost always comes down to three-strand twisted or double-braid. The following criteria are listed as an aid to making the choice between twisted or braided rope:

• Twisted rope is less expensive than double-braid rope of the same size, fiber, and quality.

• Twisted rope is more elastic than braided rope.

• Twisted rope is much easier to splice than braid-on-braid.

• Several types of splices and knots are possible in twisted rope that cannot be done in braid (i.e., end knots such as manrope and Matthew Walker, and short splicing into the middle of a length).

• Braided rope, size for size, is stronger.

• Double-braid can be spliced to 7x19 wire cable. The splice is durable and strong, which is not true of three-strand rope-to-wire splices.

• Braid runs through blocks better.

• Braid holds most knots better.

• Braid winches better because it has more contact with drum.

• Braided rope works in sheet stoppers much better than twisted rope.

• Braid will not hockle or generate a torque under load.

• Braid is less elastic than twisted rope.

Wire Cable Materials

Wire cable for yachting applications is available in two different alloys. By far the most frequently used — the standard material — is type 302/304 stainless steel. It provides the best combination of tensile strength and resistance to corrosion consistent with reasonable cost. The other alloy, type 316 stainless, offers a tradeoff — higher corrosion resistance for about 10 percent lower breaking strength and substantially higher cost.

Wire Cable Construction

Wires, being long and narrow cylinders, pack together in certain geometrical patterns (see figure C). Only three geometries of wire cable are used on modern yachts: 1x19, 7x7, and 7x19. In each case, the first number refers to the number of strands which are twisted together to make up the cable, and the second number is the number of wires in each strand.

The simplest of the patterns found in cables used on yachts consists of a central wire with six others around it for a total of seven (1x7). Each of the strands of 7x7 is made up of seven wires arranged this way (1x7), and the seven strands that make up the cable follow the same geometry. Another circle of 12 wires can be added around the circle of six to give 19 wires as in 1x19 cable. Seven-by-nineteen cable is made up of seven such 1x19 strands, for a total of 133 wires.

With wire cable, another physical property becomes important — flexibility, or the ability to withstand lateral bending without damage. Breakage due to metal fatigue caused by lack of flexibility is the major deterioration prob-

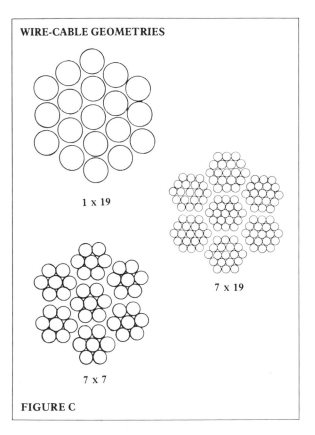

WIRE-CABLE GEOMETRIES

1 x 19

7 x 19

7 x 7

FIGURE C

lem with cable (and a safety hazard as well — broken wires are dangerous).

The flexibility of wire cable depends on the metal the wires are made of and on the diameter of the wires. Almost all cables used on yachts are type 304 stainless steel, so that the wire diameter becomes the primary variable on which flexibility depends. On yachts, the problem of cable flexibility usually relates to the size of the radius which a cable can turn around a block or sheave without being significantly weakened. For type 304 cable, sheave radius should not be less than 125 times the diameter of the wire from which the cable is made. The wires in 1x19 cable have a diameter of one-fifth of that of the cable; for 7x7 the fraction is one-ninth;

181

for 7x19, one-fifteenth. Let us work out the minimum sheave radius for ¼-inch 1x19 cable. The wire diameter is one-fifth of ¼ inch, or .05 inches. One hundred twenty-five times that diameter is 6¼ inches. (This clearly eliminates 1x19 cable from any application where it will actually be passing over a sheave: it is simply not flexible enough.)

Using the same arithmetic, we find the minimum sheave radius for ¼-inch 7x7 cable is 3½ inches; that for ¼-inch 7x19 is about two inches. Theoretically, this calls into question the common practice of splicing halyard ends around thimbles (which have considerably smaller diameters). In practice, halyards never fail at the thimble; they go above the thimble. It is the action of the cable repeatedly bending and straightening as it runs over the sheave that causes metal fatigue and failure. Cable spliced around a thimble is bent only once and never moves again.

Uses of Wire Cable

Wire cables are appropriate for several rigging applications due to their low elasticity and their abrasion resistance. Among the three types there is a direct relationship between elasticity and flexibility: 1x19 is the least elastic and the least flexible; 7x19 is the most elastic and the most flexible; 7x7 is slightly more elastic and considerably more flexible than 1x19.

In standing rigging attached with terminals, where very little flexibility is needed and elasticity is clearly undesirable, 1x19 cable is the appropriate material. If the ends of standing rigging are to be turned around thimbles, 7x7 is used due to its substantially greater flexibility. Its increased elasticity is compensated for in other ways. Seven-by-

seven is also good for lifelines, which must be somewhat more flexible than stays and shrouds. Halyards require very flexible cordage, and the only wire cable that meets this criterion is 7x19. Seven-by-nineteen can also be used for lifelines and, in fact, it can even be used for standing rigging as it was on my sloop IPHISA. Structural elongation of 7x19 cable is substantial — about four inches in a 100-foot length of ¼-inch, type 304 cable — and this has to be taken up after the first few sails if lee shrouds are not to go very slack. The ease of working with 7x19 cable — of splicing and of attaching it using swaged sleeves (see page 140) — may carry enough weight with some sailors to cause them to choose it for standing rigging.

Wire Cable Defects

Most defects in wire cable appear to originate with the preforming process. If wire is properly preformed, it lies evenly and there are no gaps. Often 1x19 wire will have a gap between two strands that can be followed for the entire length of the piece. This occurs where one or more of the wires was overformed. It will never lie properly and the individual wires in the cable are certain to be unevenly loaded. Wire cable should be carefully inspected before purchase and any but perfect rejected.

Rod Rigging

The search for stronger and stiffer standing rigging has led inevitably to the use of solid structures, namely metal rods, which are really no more than wires of the appropriate diameter and material used singly rather than twisted into a cable. Rod rigging is a comparatively new development in yachting.

It is used on the hottest racers, and is now standard equipment on some of the best production boats, and on many custom designs.

The metal selected for rod rigging is critical. Since the structure of the rod provides virtually no elasticity, it follows that any elasticity present will be due to the physical properties of the alloy used. Since standing rigging is subjected to continual dynamic loading, it would seem logical to select an alloy that has maximum elasticity consistent with high tensile strength. Most of the rod rigging in use today is made of Armco Nitronic 50, which has about the same strength and density as type 304 steel but much greater elasticity. Twelve-meter boats and a few other "extreme machines" use rod of a cobalt alloy that is more than twice as strong, reducing weight aloft but costing 10 times as much.

The eternal problem of attaching the ends of rigging is solved in one of three ways with rod: either a swage-on fitting is pressed on a knurled rod end, a Norseman mechanical terminal used, or the end is cold-headed, meaning that it is pressured into a greater diameter (about double that of the rod) that is then too large to escape from the bore of special end fittings.

Swage-on ends are as unsatisfactory for rod as they are for 1x19 wire cable. In addition to the usual swage problems, rod can be (and therefore will be) loaded more heavily than cable, applying greater stress to the swaged joint than in the case of cable, and probably leading to earlier failure. Navtec, Inc., which sells the patented machinery for the cold-heading process, also manufactures an excellent line of end fittings for rod. These are described in the chapter on terminals and end fittings.

Armco supplies rod in rolls of 30-inch diameter, so that the pieces must be straightened before installation. Rod is about 20 times less flexible than 1x19 wire of the same diameter, making a special straightening machine indispensable. (Navtec supplies such machines.) Once straightened, the rod can be rolled into an eight-foot-diameter coil for shipping or storage if it is not possible to keep it straight. Even bending it to this four-foot radius, however, will introduce a curvature which, though not harmful, is unsightly and cannot be removed even by turnbuckle tension.

Rod versus Wire Cable Rigging

Diameter for diameter, rod is stronger than cable since it is solid in cross section. (In a wire cable of the same diameter, a significant portion of the cross-sectional area consists of voids between the wires.) Rod rigging has very low elasticity — 30 percent below 1x19 wire of the same diameter. This means that a rod headstay will deflect 30 percent less under a lateral load from a sail than a wire-cable stay at the same tension. A significant improvement in windward ability results.

Rod rigging reduces windage over wire cable, since smaller diameters can be used. The smoothness of rod also contributes to the reduction of windage, as well as virtually eliminating chafe with sails, sheets, and jib hanks. Windage can be even further reduced by rolling rod into an elliptical or lenticular section for shrouds and backstays (headstays must be round to carry hanks).

Rod rigging should last forever. Corrosion is almost absent because the alloy is resistant and the surface area is minimal (wire cable corrodes primarily on the inside). Fatigue,

183

the most serious potential problem, can be largely eliminated by well-designed toggled end fittings.

The disadvantages of rod are increased initial cost, difficulty of transportation and storage, and the necessity of expensive custom machines for assembly. Rod is roughly 60 percent more expensive than type 304 wire with mechanical ends. Since this is far and away the most common rig, this is the most significant comparison. I believe that the advantages of rod are worth the extra money and that the added cost will probably be recouped when the boat is sold, or, if she is kept indefinitely, by not re-rigging.

Chain Construction

Chain is made in a vast and confusing array of shapes and sizes. The nominal sizes of chain refer to the diameter of the rod that was used to make up the links, so that the width of links is more than three times the nominal diameter.

The length of links is quite variable, but most chain used on yachts has links about six times the nominal diameter. The length of links is a compromise between the tendency of short-link chain to jam itself into hockles and of long-link chain to bend links when rounding a gypsy or roller under load. Stud-link chain, in which a bar is welded across each link, is substantially stronger than regular chain because the bar opposes the force pushing the sides of links together when the chain is under tension; but it is not generally available in sizes smaller than $^{7}/_{16}$ inch.

Most chain is made of galvanized (zinc-coated) mild steel. The quality of the steel and of the welds varies widely, as is shown by

the range of breaking strengths (see Table, p. 215). The quality of galvanizing is also extremely variable. Some chain starts to bleed and to leave rust stains on the deck after just a few uses, yet I have had galvanized-chain anchor rode that was in heavy use for seven years without significant rusting.

Steel chain in terms of material properties, like steel rod, is virtually without elasticity. If a length of chain is stretched vertically between two points and then subjected to a sufficient load, it will break. If it is suspended horizontally, however, it gains something analogous to elasticity by virtue of its weight and the more or less infinite flexibility imparted to it by its structure: it hangs down in an arc, called a "catenary," which exerts force on the points of attachment. In effect, the weight of the chain opposes and balances the forces pulling its ends apart. (To remove all of the arc, the forces pulling on the chain would have to be infinite. This is another example of lateral load effect.) The most frequent application of chain on boats —its use as anchor rode —takes full advantage of this principle, which is discussed more fully in the following chapter.

Deterioration

Virtually every item on a boat has a limited useful life; more often than not it is 10 years or less. Made right, at great expense or effort, some gear will last indefinitely, but this is *not* true for any kind of line, cable, or chain. Their deterioration is inevitable, so they must be considered expendable from the start. This is seldom understood, however, and rigging and ground tackle are often used well beyond their safe life expectancy. Useful data on most kinds of deterioration are not available, so that the discussion and recommendations which follow are of necessity incomplete and somewhat speculative.

The major causes of deterioration in synthetic fiber ropes are ultraviolet radiation, knotting, and chafing. Wire cables suffer from fatigue and oxidation, whereas fatigue appears to be the only significant cause of deterioration in rod rigging. Galvanized chain oxidizes rapidly in marine situations if the coating is worn.

Ultraviolet Degradation

Ultraviolet radiation causes the deterioration of synthetic fibers for the same reason it causes sunburn — some kinds of chemical bonds can absorb UV and be destroyed as a result. Different polymers have differing resistance to UV degradation depending on how many susceptible chemical bonds are present. Polypropylene appears to degrade much more rapidly in sunlight than nylon or Dacron.

Synthetic ropes can be protected from UV damage by pigments and special chemical UV inhibitors. These substances absorb UV and convert it to heat, which, within limits, cannot harm the fibers. Polypropylene rope made without UV inhibitors deteriorates very rapidly. Black rope is very desirable on boats because it lasts longer. Unfortunately, it is rarely available. When there is a choice, always pick the darker-colored rope — it will definitely last longer. If more sailors were aware of the advantages of black rope — if there were greater demand — more of it would be manufactured.

Chafing

Any rope that is used is subject to friction, which will eventually wear it out. In the most extreme cases of severe chafe, the destruction can occur very rapidly. Slower deterioration results from routine use such as loading, knotting, cleating, running over sheaves, and the like. Used rope can be considerably weaker than new even though little wear is apparent.

Yachtsmen should retire ropes from critical applications long before they usually do. Halyards and topping lifts can be made into deck lashings, and mooring pendants into spring lines, where their failure will not endanger life, limb, or boat.

185

Chafe occurs whenever line rubs against anything. Lines in use must be frequently inspected for chafe and the causes of chafe eliminated. Anchor and dock lines often rub on rails and chocks. At these points they should be protected with fabric wrappings, plastic tubing, or rubber guards. Rope can also chafe against other rope; dock lines should be carefully rigged to avoid such contact. Halyards can chafe against sheaves and masthead fittings. Often, serious chafing occurs because of sharp edges and other irregularities, which can be smoothed off with file and sandpaper.

All recurring chafe problems demand permanent solutions. The two most useful permanent solutions are plastic hose and chain. Clear plastic hose is available in sizes which can be slipped over dock lines and mooring pendants before splicing. Always make the hoses longer than seems necessary — a situation will inevitably arise where the extra protection is useful. Eye splices on dock lines can be made up with tubing to avoid chafe from the motley assortment of cleats, posts, and pilings one is required to use. If you keep your boat at a permanent slip, lines can be made up with thimbled eye splices which are shackled to short chains on the cleats or pilings. Mooring-pendant chafe on a bow roller or its ears can be eliminated by attaching a short chain to the pendant and a rope tail to the other chain end. The rope tail can be cleated down or can have an eye splice to go over a post or cleat. Many chocks are too small to accept lines with anti-chafe tubing; install larger chocks.

As I have mentioned several times, there is a special chafing problem with nylon rope which all sailors should be concerned about. Nylon is very elastic, and in almost any application where it touches anything be-

tween its points of attachment, such as a chock between a cleat and an anchor, it will chafe severely as its elongation changes with varying load. Nylon lines should be carefully protected from chafe wherever they contact a chock, rail, stanchion, or anything else.

Corrosion

Comments on resistance to acids and bases often appear in rope-advertising literature. All of the synthetic fibers are moderately resistant to anything likely to be used on a boat. As a general practice it is wise to keep solutions such as the phosphoric acid products used to remove rust stains away from ropes.

Corrosion is a constant and serious problem with nonstainless wire cable, but since the latter is virtually obsolete I will leave readers who are concerned with this matter to check the more classic manuals, such as Hiscock's fine books, which are full of traditional remedies.

Almost all 1x19 rigging cable shows at least some discoloration within a few years. There is enormous variation in how much change takes place, which is confusing because type 302/304 alloys are used almost exclusively. An occasional boat is rigged with 316 alloy cable, but this is strictly a special-order job. Experts disagree on the causes of this discoloration, but they seem to agree that it is harmless and does not reduce the strength of the cable.

The Nitronic 50 alloy used by Navtec is more corrosion-resistant than 316 stainless, and there is much less surface to support corrosion on a rod than with 1x19 cable; hence, corrosion should never constitute a serious problem with rod.

Fatigue

Fatigue is the major deterioration problem with wire cables. The surest sign of fatigue in wire cables is broken wires, aptly called "meathooks." Wire breaks almost always occur where the cable rides on a sheave. These areas should be regularly inspected. When any wire breaks, the entire cable should be replaced as soon as possible and the cause of the fatigue remedied if possible. In 1x19 standing rigging, fatigue occurs when the ends are inadequately toggled and so not free to move, or because the shrouds are loose and go slack on the lee side. Wire breaks on 1x19 stays almost always occur at the terminals.

Headstays are especially prone to fatigue due to the lateral load from headsails. It is essential that headstays be properly toggled top and bottom. Meathooks sometimes develop in 7x19 halyards because the head of the jib is too free and falls off. This problem can be solved with an extra jib hank near the head thimble.

Rod rigging appears to be very long-lasting if handled properly (it has yet to stand the test of time). Without proper toggles, however, rod will probably not last as long as 1x19 wire — being less flexible, it is more subject to fatigue. Adequate tension is essential to counter fatigue with rod. If shrouds are loose enough to go slack on the lee side, fatigue can be serious enough to cause failure.

Both with rod and 1x19 wire, it is advisable to use a tension gauge when taking up on turnbuckles, both to equalize tensions on either side of the rig and to avoid overloading.

"Meathooks," the broken wires shown here on the 7x7-cable halyard, are the result of metal fatigue.

Safety Factors

Hydraulic press at the Cordage Institute used to determine the breaking strength of ropes.

Safety factor is the ratio between the load at which cordage is strained to its elastic limit, and working load — the maximum load to which we expect it to be subjected. Almost everything discussed in this chapter is summarized in this number. Let us start with breaking strength and review the reasoning by which we might arrive at a working load and, hence, a safety factor for a given rope.

Breaking strength is the tension at which samples failed when tested. Working load cannot approach this tension or damage to the cordage will surely result. Let us start with a sample of rope with breaking strength

of 1,000 pounds and assume its elastic limit to be 600 pounds. On a testing machine in a test lab, this sample could be loaded repeatedly to 600 pounds and last almost indefinitely — the sample has proper eye splices placed over large, smooth capstans and does not come into contact with anything that might cause chafe.

The deck of a yacht is obviously a very different environment, and ropes are subjected to many abuses not encountered in the test lab. Probably the four most important of these are chafe, photochemical degradation, knots, and running over blocks and sheaves.

188

In order to insure reasonable longevity, it is necessary to increase the safety factor — make the work load a fraction of the elastic limit.

Smaller ropes have greater surface area relative to their cross-sectional areas than larger ropes. Chafe and photochemical degradation affect the rope surface, so that smaller ropes, with relatively large surface areas, require larger safety factors to achieve the same useful life.

Some ropes are more subject to chafe than others. Again, nylon ropes are very elastic, which causes them to saw back and forth on a chafe point as they are alternately stressed and relaxed, as in dock lines. (A Dacron line in the same situation will not saw nearly as much, but, of course, it will not be as efficient at absorbing dynamic loads either.) Safety factors for nylon ropes are increased to compensate for this.

Knots and poorly made splices reduce the breaking strength of a piece of rope. As they are regular occurrences on most yachts, safety factors must be increased to account for them. A seaman who uses no knots and makes every splice perfectly could reduce safety factors by about a third.

The accepted system of safety factors in general usage for fiber ropes represents an attempt by the compilers to make allowances, on an empirical basis, for all the variables involved in rope deterioration due to usage. The idea is to provide guidelines for rope selection that will ensure reasonable longevity for all sizes and types of fiber ropes. The Cordage Institute publishes a chart of these safety factor findings; it is reproduced in the Appendix.

Safety factors are used for wire cables, and chain as well, but they are much closer to the ratio between breaking strength and elastic limit. The reason is that the environment has relatively little effect on the strength of these materials, and most of the things yachtsmen do to them are equally innocuous. It is important to note, however, that if cables are spliced around thimbles or sharply bent in other ways, the safety factor should be increased substantially to compensate for the weakness such bends create.

With chain anchor rodes, weight is a more critical consideration than breaking strength. It is important not to subject chain to direct dynamic loading, where its weight cannot damp the acceleration, because this almost always causes failure. I have never heard of chain breaking under any other conditions. Safety factors *per se* for chain are generally ignored.

In summary, commonly accepted safety factors represent the collective experience of many experts on what working loads result in satisfactory performance and acceptable cordage life. Under very favorable conditions or in circumstances in which known risks are deemed acceptable, smaller safety factors might be used, while critical applications and harsh environments demand larger safety factors.

Chapter 10
Structures: rigging and ground tackle

My purpose in this chapter is to consider the kinds of loads that are applied to the materials discussed in the last chapter, in their typical applications aboard boats. The aim is an understanding that can be applied to real situations. The engineering involved is quite simple and direct, so the informed yachtsman should begin to be able to easily recognize situations that can overload ropes, cables, and chain.

There are three primary reasons for rig failure: the yacht is put to harder use than it was designed for, the rig is changed in ways that make it less efficient at supporting the mast, or the rig is not properly maintained. It is not necessary for yachtsmen to know how to design standing rigging, but they should understand enough about its design so that they do not modify or abuse it in ways that reduce its efficiency.

On the other hand, all the other structures discussed in this chapter — running rigging, ground tackle, dock lines, and lifelines — *are* routinely designed by yachtsmen. Some basic insight into the principles behind all aspects of rig design should certainly help boat owners to avoid making costly and dangerous mistakes. The amateur builder or the buyer of a new yacht will also be able to put all of the information in this chapter to good use, either in choosing a design or in selecting optional equipment.

Loads on Standing Rigging

Standing rigging is pre-stressed — it is under tension before you put on the sails. The sails generate additional loads, which stress the rigging further. I use the terms "initial load" and "sailing load" for these two components, and I call their sum "total load." The initial load is easily measured or calculated. Calculating sailing load is somewhat more complicated, but reasonable approximations can be reached by fairly simple methods. The total sailing load can be divided into the load borne by the windward shrouds, and the load borne by the headstay (which is opposed by an equal load on the backstay).

Loads on Shrouds

Shrouds hold the mast upright in the hull as the force of wind against sail heels the boat. The sailing load on shrouds is the component of total sail force that causes heeling. (The thrust or forward driving force from the sails has little effect on shroud tension.) But shroud tension is only one of the components of the force that opposes heeling force — the other is mast compression. If we know the force that produces a given degree of heel (and, hence, the force that opposes it), we can calculate the resulting shroud tension. Some vector work is necessary to break down the force opposing heeling force into its components: shroud tension and mast compression. If you are not already familiar with vector addition, refer to the examples in Chapter 8.

Determining Heeling Force

Every sailboat has an optimum angle of heel that depends on the shape of the hull. Let us assume in this discussion that optimum heel

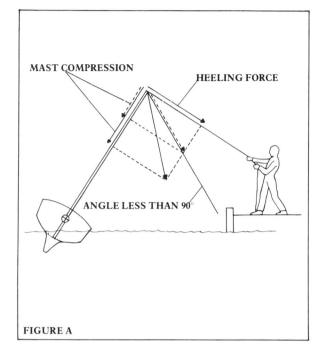

FIGURE A

Finding Shroud Tension

FIGURE B

is 25°. With the boat docked it is a simple matter to determine how much force is required to heel her over 25°. Attach a line to a masthead halyard, move as far away as the line or dock allows, and see how many men, each pulling about 50 pounds, are needed to careen the boat 25°. If the boat is normally sailed with crew hanging on hiking straps or trapeze rigs, position them for this test. One or two men can pull most monohulls under 20 feet over to optimum heel. If more force is required, rig a tackle to the careening line. If the careening line is at right angles to the mast, then the heeling force is equal to the tension on the line. If the angle is less than 90° (it is not likely to be more), part of the careening-line tension is compressing the mast, and a vector addition will have to be done to determine how much force is heeling the boat. Figure A shows how to set up this vector problem.

Once we know what the heeling force is, we must figure out how it is distributed. If we are dealing with a rig with single shrouds, then the entire force of heeling is opposed by tension on the windward shroud. Another vector addition has to be done to determine the shroud tension necessary to oppose the heeling force. Figure B shows how to convert heeling force into actual load on the single windward shroud. Most modern rigs have three shrouds on each side — single upper shrouds and double lower shrouds, with the lowers attached halfway up the mast, immediately below the spreaders. The heeling force is divided up among these three shrouds, so that about half is on the upper and the other half on the two lowers. Since the lower shrouds are attached only half the distance from the center of rotation, twice the tension is needed to oppose the same amount of force applied at the masthead. Thus, the three shrouds can be assumed to be under equal sailing loads, each opposing one-half of the heeling force at the masthead, as

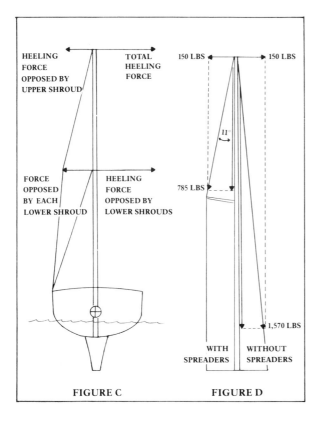

FIGURE C   FIGURE D

pounds at the masthead, directed abeam and at right angles to the mast, to heel her over 25°. Thus the upper and each of the lower shrouds have to oppose about 150 pounds of this force at a lead angle of approximately 11° (see figure D). The vector addition shows the sailing-load tension on each of the shrouds to amount to about 785 pounds.

Initial Shroud Load

Initial shroud load is adjusted by means of turnbuckles. The initial load should be just sufficient so that the lee shrouds do not go slack under sail. Slack lee shrouds will be subject to metal fatigue and will eventually fail. There is no advantage to loading shrouds beyond what is needed to keep them from going slack. Tightening beyond this point simply cuts into the reserve capacity of the shrouds to absorb any extraordinary shock load, such as might occur in a knockdown or when some piece of running rigging fails: i.e., your safety factor. There is another important danger from loose shrouds, aside from the fatigue problem, and that is that the mast will move about, chewing into its step. In cases of extreme slackness, the mast may accelerate enough to subject the rigging to substantial dynamic loads.

Initial shroud loads may be found either by using a tension gauge, or by figuring the mechanical advantage of the lever arms you use to tighten your turnbuckles and estimating the force you are exerting in turning them. Care must be taken that the combined initial and sailing loads do not exceed 50 percent of the working load of the rigging material, or about 20 percent of its breaking strength.

shown in figure C. Once we know this, the sailing load on each shroud can be calculated as in the single-shroud example (figure B).

Figure D illustrates how spreaders reduce the sailing load on upper shrouds as well as reducing mast compression. This analysis applies equally to double-spreader rigs: the load on the upper shroud is one-third of the heeling force, and the load on the interme-diate shroud and on each of the two lower shrouds is one-half of the heeling force. Rigs with more than one mast can be analyzed by dividing the heeling force among the masts in proportion to the sail area each carries.

Speed tests, carried out under various conditions of wind and sea, have shown CYCLURA's optimum close-hauled sailing stance to be 25° of heel. It takes about 300

Loads on Headstays

Headstays are a special problem because the sails attached to them exert lateral loads, causing the stays to sag to windward. This constitutes a problem because, while most sailors seem to be aware of the theoretical advantages of a straight luff in terms of sail efficiency, few seem to understand the dangers of overtightening their stays in attempting to eliminate the inevitable sag. (We know from our previous discussion of lateral loads (see Chapter 8) that *any* lateral load from the jib will produce *some* deflection.) The more we increase initial tension in an attempt to reduce lateral deflection — in other words, the less deflection we allow — the more the lateral load is multiplied. As the inital load increases, the total tension in the stay opposing the lateral load increases sharply. The factor limiting attempts to compensate for headstay sag is the breaking strength of the rigging material — it is not as hard to exceed this as many yachtsmen believe.

Because the load is not evenly distributed, but rather concentrated towards the middle of the stay, the mathematics needed to precisely analyze it are extremely complicated; a simplified model should provide insight and allow us to arrive at approximate solutions. On many modern sloops, it is reasonable to assume that the entire heeling force is communicated to the mast through the headstay. If we further assume that the entire thrust is transmitted through the sheet, and the heeling force acts on the midpoint of the stay, we can draw a vector diagram (see figure E).

Based on this simplified model, I have worked out a table relating the degree of deflection on a stay to the ratio between the lateral load and the total stay tension pro- duced by it. For example, if a lateral load of *x* pounds produces a deflection of 1°, the total tension exerted by that stay in opposing the lateral load will be 28.7 times *x*. If *x* produces a 2° deflection, clearly the stay is somewhat slacker and the lateral-load effect will be smaller — total tension will be 14.4 times *x*. For other degrees of deflection, refer to the table accompanying figure E.

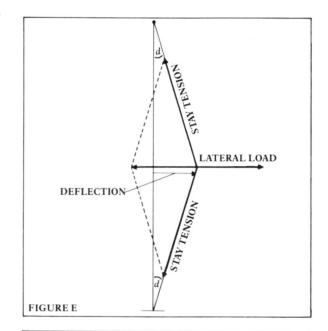

FIGURE E

HEADSTAY DEFLECTION RELATED TO TOTAL HEADSTAY TENSION	
Deflection Angle (d)	**Total Stay Tension** **Lateral Load**
0.25°	114.6
0.5°	57.3
1.0°	28.7
2.0°	14.4
3.0°	9.5
4.0°	7.2
5.0°	5.75
6.0°	4.75

Lateral deflection, then, is an index to initial stay tension. But it gives us also an empirical method by which to get a ball-park estimate of total loads. If I know, for example, that the maximum headsail load I can expect under normal conditions is 500 pounds, and I know the working load of my stay, I can find out how little deflection or sag I can get away with at that load, and tension my headstay-backstay assembly accordingly.

If the distinction between initial load and sailing load has been glossed over here, the reason is simply that while we can measure the initial tensioning of the head- and backstays using a gauge, there is no simple method of calculating the sailing load independent of it — the magnitude of the former effects the magnitude of the latter.

Headstays and backstays operate in opposition to each other. Headstay load equals backstay load, but unless the two stays make the same angle with the mast, the *tensions* will *not* be equal. Whichever stay makes the smaller angle with the mast (usually the headstay) will require greater tension to balance the load exerted by the other (see figure F). This is important since any load placed on the backstay will be transferred to the headstay in the same proportion. If headstay tension in equilibrium is $1.5 \times$ backstay tension, a load of x pounds placed on the backstay will be transferred to the headstay as a load of $1.5\ x$.

Design and Maintenance of Standing Rigging

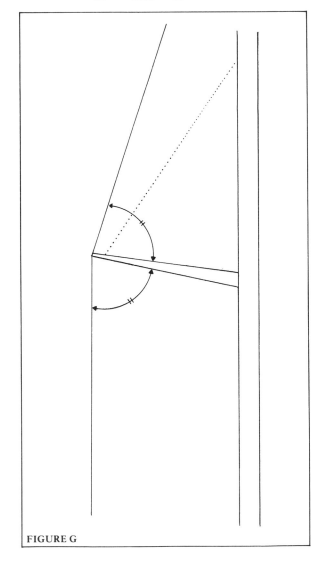

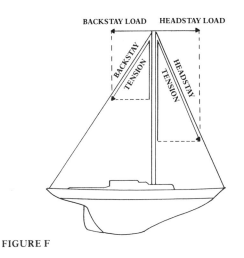

BACKSTAY LOAD   HEADSTAY LOAD

FIGURE F

FIGURE G

Upper Shrouds and Spreaders. One of the more common causes of rig failure is the collapse of the windward spreader. To function properly, the spreader must bisect the bend angle of the upper shroud, so that it is under compression only and not bent (see figure G). These angles need not be precisely measured, but any deviation which is evident to the naked eye should be corrected. Boats with sagging spreaders can be seen at any marina—some sagging below the horizontal. Upper-shroud tension exerts a bending force on sagging spreaders which increases under sail load. No spreaders are designed to oppose a substantial bend, so failure of sagging spreaders is predictable. Spreader tips should be supported in their proper positions on the shrouds. There are several systems which work equally well. The spreader can be attached to the appropriate point on the shroud by a lashing or, in the case of rod rigging, by a spreader-bend fitting. On CYCLURA, the spreader-mounting brackets on the mast support the spreader at the appropriate angle. Many older yachts used a short support wire from the masthead, sometimes with turnbuckle, to hold spreaders up (see dotted line in figure G). Such wires cause unnecessary windage and seem the least desirable solution.

Spreaders also fail due to lack of maintenance. Many sailors who religiously inspect their standing rigging never examine their spreaders. Wooden spreaders mounted in metal box brackets tend to rot at the base. Spreader brackets screwed onto wooden masts sometimes fall off because the screw holes rot. Aluminum spreaders are often poorly designed; their mounting holes tend to widen until the spreaders fall off their brackets. The same result can occur with alloy spars if the screws or rivets shear from excessive spreader motion. Some types of spreader tips are known to become disassociated from the shroud.

When buying new equipment, carefully consider how these problems are met by the design. When inspecting rigging, pay close attention to spreaders. While under sail, look at the windward spreader regularly—many a rig has been saved by an alert helmsman, tacking after having noticed incipient failure.

Headstays. As discussed earlier, headstays are more heavily loaded than other standing rigging because of the lateral forces generated by headsails. (The same is true of any other stay which carries a sail.) Because of the vulnerability of headstays, the ocean-cruising yachtsman should have a fail-safe system. On CYCLURA, I have rigged twin headstays to a triangular plate connected to the stem fitting by a single oversized turnbuckle. In addition, I carry an inner forestay rigged at all times, and I do not fly any really large genoas. My forestays are quite slack, but this has not prevented fast passage—making (183 nautical miles in 24 hours is my current record).

Many older yachts have been modernized by removal of the bowsprit. A headstay moved to the stem will make a smaller angle with the mast and thus be under greater tension. Such modifications should probably always include using a larger size of wire for the stay. Many racer/cruisers which are never raced would also benefit from larger wire on the forestay.

Besides making sure that the materials—the cable or rod and associated hardware—are sufficiently strong to bear the forces encountered, the design of head- and backstays relates to the means provided for adjusting tension. This will be discussed a little further on.

197

Safety Factors. The safety factors allowed for standing rigging should vary according to the usage to which the yacht in question will be put. Hobie Cats, for example, are very lightly rigged for top performance in light airs. This is appropriate for small lakes and other protected areas where these catamarans are most often sailed. In the Virgin Islands, however, the rig regularly fails. Usually, little damage is done, and the whole thing can be put back together with a few new stays. This is not the case with larger yachts where the disaster of dismasting is to be avoided if at all possible. I assume that the smallest safety factor any designer would use for standing rigging is *three,* since at 40 percent of breaking strength 7 x 19 stainless cable undergoes plastic deformation. With rod rigging, this safety factor (ratio between breaking strength and working load) might be reduced to *two* in the case of the most competitive racers. These low safety factors are chosen to win races, not to keep the rig in the boat indefinitely. A casual racer with a lightly rigged boat should increase the safety factor to about *four.* Any yachts which go offshore, whether for racing or pleasure, should apply safety factors of at least *five* to their rigging. A good principle for ocean cruisers is that if the rigging does not look too big, it is too small. There are advocates of light-and-fast everything for offshore yachts, but I have seen many serious failures on such yachts sailing *inshore,* which offshore would have been life-threatening. I can enjoy passages on CYCLURA largely because I am confident that nothing will break.

Hardware. Standing rigging is attached to mast fittings and chainplates. Make sure that they are strong enough. The standard practice is to make turnbuckles, terminals, and

everything else stronger than the wire. My practice is to know the strength of everything I use and to avoid overloading the weakest link. In-use inspection is essential. Even slight deformation often indicates forthcoming failure. Elongated clevis-pin holes in tangs and chainplates, for example, show that they are not strong enough for the loads applied.

Terminals. The failure of a terminal has essentially the same consequences as the breaking of a stay or the failure of a spreader. Terminals should be inspected regularly, most especially tube-type swage-on terminals which definitely have a limited life.

Fatigue. The two causes of fatigue are first, that a cable or fitting is not free to lead true, and second, that a cable or fitting regularly loses tension and flails about. The solution to the first problem is to toggle every piece of standing rigging top and bottom. A common mistake is to toggle only the lower end of a headstay, while attaching the upper end to the masthead in such a way that any deflection bends the wire as it exits from the terminal fitting. Such rigs are very short-lived indeed.

My philosophy on rigging tension is that it should be tight enough so that it never goes slack. Slack rigging whips about, bending and fatiguing both wire and fittings.

Excessive Tension. Rigging which is too tight may be near the elastic limit of the wire or rod. Extra loads, such as those caused by pounding in a seaway, may surpass the elastic limit and produce permanent elongation. The devotee of tight rigging will then screw the turnbuckles down tighter and pull the wire out some more. Eventually, the wire will be weakened to an extent that makes

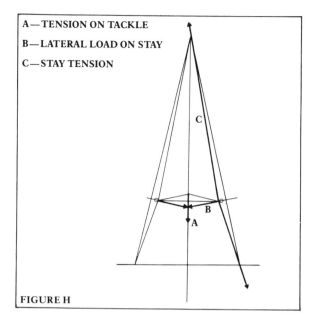

A—TENSION ON TACKLE

B—LATERAL LOAD ON STAY

C—STAY TENSION

FIGURE H

failure inevitable. Turnbuckles of the proper size for rigging have the advantage that it is difficult to overtighten them without using a lever arm that is clearly excessive.

Many of the devices available for adjusting backstays are not limited this way, and overtensioning can frequently be brought about with little effort. I am especially alarmed by the tackles attached to a pair of blocks which pull twin backstays together. The vector analysis in figure H shows my cause for concern. The problem is similar to that of headstays — a relatively small lateral load on a pre-tensioned wire deflects it slightly and greatly increases its tension. I have attempted to draw figure H to a realistic scale. If a four-part tackle is used, exerting a lateral load of 200 pounds, a backstay tension greater than 12,000 pounds results with the angles shown — well in excess of the breaking strengths of backstays on the light and racy 30-footers which use this kind of device.

The backstay tensioners with levers or

wheels, or the geared type, which uses a winch handle, are probably safer in this regard because they do not provide such excessive mechanical advantage. Anyone planning to install one of these stay-tensioners, however, should determine the mechanical advantage by measuring the change in the length of the stay for each turn of the handle or wheel. If, for example, we are using the geared type of adjustor with a 10-inch winch handle, which turns 63 inches in one turn, and the change in stay length is ½ inch, the mechanical advantage is 126-to-1. A 50-pound effort on the handle would yield a 6,300-pound tension, which should not be applied to wire cable smaller than ⅜ inch in diameter.

Turnbuckles and the other mechanical devices used as tension adjustors do not adjust tension *per se*; they regulate the *length* of the forestay/backstay assembly. In situations where rigs are tuned very tightly for maximum sail efficiency, there is always danger of failure if unexpected stresses should occur, since these mechanisms provide no kind of relief or safety valve to fall back on.

Headstay/backstay tension *cannot* be optimized, but there *is* one way to achieve the best possible compromise while eliminating the danger of overloading the rig: the use of a hydraulic tension adjustor. This device, usually referred to as the "hydraulic backstay adjustor," does respond to the actual rig tension, making adjustments automatically as needed while maintaining maximum allowable tension at all times. It has relief valves that are set for a reasonable, predetermined load (the working load of the rigging). So, with a properly set and properly functioning hydraulic adjustor, safe loads *cannot* be exceeded.

Tuning Standing Rigging

The objective of tuning standing rigging is to keep the mast straight while the boat is under sail. Tuning is accomplished by adjusting turnbuckles and sighting up the mainsail track. On the first cycle of tuning (these cycles can continue indefinitely), no effort should be made to get the rigging very tight. Once the mast is straight at the dock, take the boat for a sail. At this stage the rigging will probably be too loose, which is shown by the lee shrouds going slack. If this is the case, take up a few turns on the lee side, then tack and tighten the same number of turns on the opposite side. Continue this routine until lee shrouds no longer go slack. It is important not to overload the rigging, which is especially easy to do with the smaller sizes of cable. Compute the mechanical advantage of different lever arms applied to your turnbuckles, and limit yourself to a lever arm which can exert no more than one-third of the breaking strength of the cable. If, with this leverage, the lee shrouds still go slack, you probably have a flexible hull or mast and should probably seek the advice of a professional surveyor. Hull or mast problems cannot be solved by overloading the standing rigging.

Once the shrouds have been tightened enough to prevent the lee side from going slack, sight up the mainsail track while close-hauled. You will probably observe the upper portion of the mast, above the spreaders, bending to leeward. This is because the upper and lower shrouds carry the same load, but the uppers, being about twice as long, elongate twice as much. Some of this differential-elongation effect has already been counteracted by taking up enough to keep the lee shrouds from going slack, but

the uppers will probably have to be tightened a few turns more.

The tuning of head- and backstays, aside from questions of tension adjustments carried out under sail, involves balancing the initial tensions so as to eliminate any mast rake — to make the mast stand perpendicular in the fore-and-aft plane. (It should be noted here, however, that some mast rake is a deliberate design feature of some boats.)

Loads on Running Rigging

On fore-and-aft rigs, the principal running rigging consists of the halyards and sheets that hold the sails in place and in shape. Several other items of running rigging, such as preventers, vangs, lifts, and guys, may be used occasionally.

Calculating loads on running rigging from a consideration of the forces acting on sails is a complicated problem and attempts to do so with precision should be left to engineers and the designers of yachts. A brief examination of the mechanics involved, however, should provide useful background for practical understanding of rigging problems.

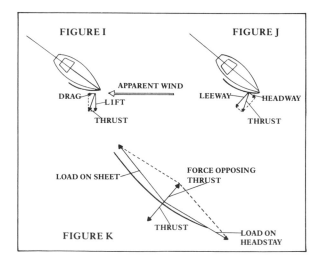

Sails are airfoils, as are airplane wings. As they move through the air, they generate two forces—*lift* and *drag* (see figure I). Lift operates perpendicular to the direction of the air flow; drag operates in the direction of the air flow. Each point on a sail has its own lift and drag. These can be summed and visualized in the mind's eye as two vectors originating at the sail's center of effort. The lift generated by a sail is much greater than the drag, so that the vector sum of the two — the thrust — is fairly close in magnitude to the lift alone. Thrust can also be broken down into two component vectors, one in the direction of the boat's course and the other perpendicular to it (see figure J). These components are commonly referred to as "headway" and "leeway"; the former drives the boat forward and the latter heels it and drives it sideways. It should be clear from this that sails generate considerably more force than what actually drives the boat forward.

The sail maintains its shape because the headstay, halyard, and sheet are under tension opposing the thrust. The sum of their tensions constitutes a vector equal and opposite to the thrust, and this may, in turn, be analyzed into two component vectors; one in the direction of the sheet and one in the direction of the headstay. Due to the angles involved, these structures oppose the thrust very inefficiently when the sail is close-hauled, and the vectors are both considerably larger than the thrust (see figure K). This is one more case of the great effect of lateral loads. (See also the simplified lateral-load example involving jibsheets, p. 169.)

There are two simple ways to measure sheet and halyard loads in practice. The first is the use of a tension gauge. A gauge that has maximum reading of at least one-half the breaking strength of the halyard or sheet to be measured can be used under sail. For halyard tension, the gauge is attached between the tack and stem, and the sail raised and trimmed normally. To measure sheet load, attach the gauge to the track or rail near the sheet lead, and run a line from the gauge to the clew. The sheet can then be eased, and the load transferred to the gauge. The measurements should be made in the strongest winds in which the boat is unreefed.

The second method is not as exact, but it does not require a tension gauge and gives an estimate close enough to be useful. All that is done is to relate the winching force to the sheet or halyard load. In the ideal case, one manpower, applied through the mechanical advantage of a winch, is just adequate to trim a sheet when it is under the greatest tension encountered. The mechanical advantage of the winch is looked up or calculated and the sheet load estimated by multiplying it by 50 pounds. If the winch is slightly inadequate, so that a bit of body bracing and extra exertion are needed, multiply by 100 pounds. Halyard load can be found by the same method, except that few boats have halyard winches that can harden up a full sail in a stiff breeze. In many cases, the halyard can be temporarily led through a snatch block to a windward-sheet winch for the purpose of this test.

Mainsheets present special load problems because of the angles involved. This is yet another case of lateral loading. The reason mainsheets almost always use tackles is to distribute the loading of the sheet, so that the rope can be of reasonable diameter. CYCLURA's mainsheet is a five-part tackle to three bails at mid-boom. The entire load, which probably exceeds 1,000 pounds at times, is carried by a large traveler on the

cabin top. Each part of the mainsheet tackle carries slightly more than one-fifth of the total load, for a maximum of about 200 pounds. The entire mainsheet arrangement allows loads twice these maximums, and the winch has sufficient mechanical advantage to apply such tension.

The load on boom-end mainsheets is approximately half that on mid-boom sheets. This is because the mid-boom sheets are below the sail's center of effort, whereas the end of the boom is considerably aft and uses the boom as a lever with 2-to-1 mechanical advantage.

Design of Running Rigging

Ideally, the running rigging of any boat should be designed as a total system that includes ropes, cables, blocks, sheaves, cleats, and winches. If rope sizes are carefully matched to blocks, cleats, and other hardware, the chances of mishaps are re-duced. The mechanical advantage of all winches should be adequate to make possible the trimming of all sails under any condi-tions that may be encountered without undue exertion. On the other hand, winches should *not* be powerful enough to generate forces that will damage lines, sails, or hardware, or weaken their own mountings.

All ropes and cables should, of course, be strong enough so that their working loads will not be approached under normal usage, nor exceeded under the most severe condi-tions. Load measurements, as discussed in the previous section, should be very useful in determining safety factors.

Lead angles should be figured carefully so lines will lead fair, eliminating binding of blocks and sheaves and minimizing chafe. It would also be useful to draw vector diagrams

for all lead angles. While the lead angles do not affect sheet tension, they do determine the loads placed on turning blocks, sheaves, etc. (see example, p. 168).

I am completely convinced that internal halyards are superior to halyards led outside the mast, but one must take care to avoid a couple of potential pitfalls. First, any sharp metal exposed inside the mast is likely to quickly destroy any rope that passes over it. Second, the ends of internal halyards must be treated in such a way as to prevent their disappearing into the mast; retrieving them can be very hard work indeed. A back splice, a stopper knot, or one of the plastic spinnaker halyard-stoppers will serve this purpose.

The job of halyards and sheets is to oppose what are basically static loads: wind forces. It is true that wind forces undergo substantial changes in magnitude, but the changes are not great in comparison to the tensions at which halyards and sheets are set up in normal usage. In any case, the elasticity of nylon rope is not called for in these applica-tions — quite the opposite. It would be extremely inefficient if increased wind force caused the softening of sail trim, which is what would happen if elastic sheets and halyards were used. We want sheets and halyards to be inelastic.

Since they are run through blocks at various angles (sometimes in tackles) and are being handled constantly, the flexibility and handling quality of rope are essential proper-ties for sheets. The material of choice for sheets, then, is Dacron (polyester) rope, preferably braided, as this offers the best available combination of flexibility and in-elasticity.

For halyards, the best solution to the elasticity problem is the use of 7x19 wire cable, which is considerably less elastic than any rope of comparable strength. The traditional difficulty, handling the cable, is now easily overcome by splicing on easy-to-handle rope tails of double braid. (Wire-to-three-strand-rope splices have *never* been satisfactory; I do not recommend them. If it is necessary to fasten three-strand rope to 7x19, put an eye and thimble in the cable and eye-splice the rope to this.) The 7x19-to-braid splice is strong, reliable, and easy to make (see Chapter 3, Tail Splice). On CYCLURA, I made up all of the halyards this way. I wrap the tails around alloy drum winches and subject the splices to the entire halyard tension. This keeps the wire inside the mast where I do not have to handle it. CYCLURA's staysail halyard had to be replaced with rope because I could not find a block which would fit between the mast and the stay and through which the splice would run freely. When I do find the block, I will go back to the wire-and-rope halyard.

I have owned two boats with rope halyards, however, and have sailed on many others. Rope halyards work well if they are of sufficient diameter and the winches have adequate mechanical advantage to set them up tightly. Often neither of these criteria is met and the sails get fuller when the wind increases. In extreme cases, luff scallops develop, which indicates very inefficient sail trim. On the other hand, CYCLURA has been driven very hard in stiff breezes for more than 24 hours at a stretch without noticeable slackening of the rope staysail halyard. Rope halyards have appreciable structural elongation, and should be stretched when new. They can be left shackled to a deck fitting and set up hard.

Topping lifts, boom vangs, and preventers (fore guys) are auxiliary pieces of running rigging used to control the position of the

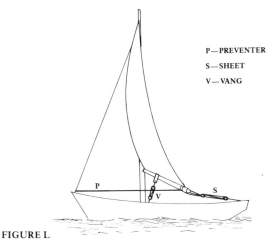

P—PREVENTER
S—SHEET
V—VANG

FIGURE L

boom. Their use is not clearly understood by a significant number of sailors; they are frequently not used when they should be, and they are often used incorrectly. There are two separate functions: to aid in trimming the mainsail in positions of sail where trimming cannot be adequately accomplished by means of the sheet alone; and to control the travel of the boom for reasons of safety.

The latter is the proper function of the preventer, or fore guy. A large, heavy wooden boom is without doubt the most potentially destructive piece of equipment on board a sailing yacht. When a boat is rolling badly, as often occurs in running, the mainsail can get badly back-winded. It is the job of the preventer, in such situations, to hold the boom athwartships, to prevent it from swinging aft; in other words, to prevent a jibe and the great dynamic loads that jibing puts on the whole rig. Most sailors are aware of the necessity of having some restraint on a boomed-out mainsail, but many are under the impression that the vang fulfills this function. A moment's consideration of the load-bearing efficiency of the lead angles will make it clear how much more efficient a preventer, properly led from the bow, is in resisting the backward swing of the boom than a vang (see figure L).

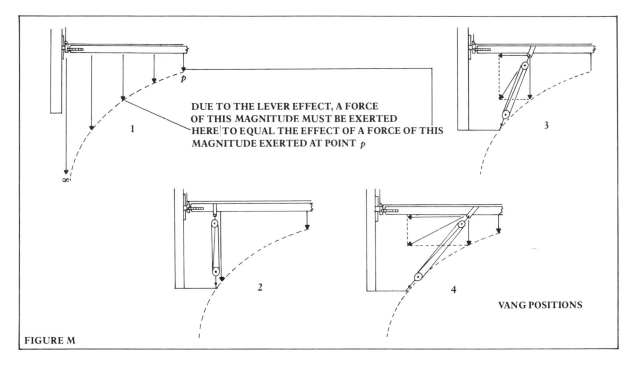

DUE TO THE LEVER EFFECT, A FORCE
OF THIS MAGNITUDE MUST BE EXERTED
HERE TO EQUAL THE EFFECT OF A FORCE OF THIS
MAGNITUDE EXERTED AT POINT *p*

VANG POSITIONS

FIGURE M

Led from the bow, a preventer opposes the backward swing of the boom in a more or less opposite direction. This eliminates lateral load problems and makes the structure efficient enough that even a relatively light line can reasonably do the job. Since it is a dynamic load that the preventer is designed to absorb, it would make sense to use nylon rope. An excellent procedure is to keep a nylon spring line rigged on the bow at all times to do double service as a preventer.

The primary function of the boom vang is to increase the efficiency of a boomed-out mainsail in strong breezes. The vang flattens the camber of the sail by hauling down on the boom. Since the boom acts as a lever, in theory, the farther out from the gooseneck the vang attaches, the greater its mechanical advantage, assuming that it is hauling straight down. Obviously, it should not attach inboard of the rail. Vang efficiency increases as its attachment points on the

boom move farther outboard, up to the point where the increase in lead angle reduces the load-bearing efficiency (lateral-load effect again) by more than the gain in leverage increases it. The optimum point of attachment must be worked out for each boat. Figure M should be useful in considering the variable relationships involved. Vangs are usually tackles of several parts. The lines used in them should probably be of nylon since the vang will inevitably be called upon, from time to time, to fulfill the function of the preventer, at least in part.

Many sailors are unaware of any function of the topping lift aside from holding up the boom when the sail is not doing so. Properly rigged, the topping lift can fulfill a number of functions. It can be used to adjust sail camber — to achieve a fuller mainsail in very light airs — by raising the boom. It can be used, in conjunction with sheets, preventer, and vang, to keep the boom firmly positioned when running in rough seas, or in any situation in which the boom's downward motion needs to be controlled. Reefing cannot be accomplished under sail without the aid of a topping lift.

The fixed and nonadjustable topping lift found on many boats is an absurd piece of rigging, since it can only be used to hold up the boom when the mainsail is furled (which is the proper function of a crutch or gallows). I prefer topping lifts that are rove through masthead sheaves and led to mast winches. If the lift is rigged in this way and made of wire cable or Dacron rope, it can serve as an auxiliary halyard — a very handy item.

Lifeline Loads and Design

The purpose of lifelines is to keep the crew on board when the forces of wind and waves are attempting to toss them overboard. It is perhaps better to have no lifelines at all than to rely on lifelines that may fail. Yachting literature is full of advice against attaching safety lines from harnesses to lifelines due to the latter's unreliability. This is the sort of reasoning that leaves me wanting to beat my head against a bulkhead. Clearly, every yacht should have *reliable* lifelines.

Terminals, fittings, and cables of lifelines should be inspected as carefully and as frequently as any standing or running rigging. Lifelines should be tested regularly, since they might otherwise go unloaded for years. My test method is to stand on the lifelines amidship and to vigorously bounce up and down, holding on to the shrouds. Many lifelines will not survive this test and should be replaced. Because of the lateral load effect, the tension exerted on the lifelines can be as great as 3,000 pounds, yet some lifelines are not even designed for such loads. Much of the so-called lifeline

hardware sold is woefully inadequate, as I discuss in Chapter 7. CYCLURA's lifelines are made up of plastic-covered 3/16-inch stainless steel 7x7 wire cable (minimum breaking strength 3,700 pounds). The ends are turned around thimbles with swaged sleeves and all the hardware is of a strength suitable for standing rigging.

Loads on Ground Tackle

The principal forces acting on ground tackle are derived from the action of wind, waves, and currents on the vessel. Other forces, such as those caused by ice, and collisions with other vessels, are not usually figured into a calculation of load but are accommodated by a generous safety factor.

The formula for calculating force resulting from drag in a fluid such as water or air is: $F = K \times A \times D \times v^2$. F is force; K is a drag coefficient with a maximum value of 1; A is the frontal area of the body; D is the density of the fluid; and v^2 is the square of the velocity of the fluid.

For a given boat, K and A will be constants. D is constant also, with different values for air and water. So again, for a given boat, the only actual variable determining mooring load is the velocity of the wind or current. Rather than attempting to make accurate assessments of all the elements in the formula, we can easily set up an empirical test to find a value for F at a given wind velocity, for example; and from this value we can determine F for any wind velocity. Try pulling your boat forward by the pendant when there is a light wind, but no waves or current. If you cannot pull the boat, wait for a lighter wind, or, if the boat moves forward very easily, wait for a stronger breeze. What you want to find is the wind velocity where

you can just inch forward. Once you are in that wind, you must estimate or measure it. You have now found the wind velocity that creates a 50-pound load on the tackle. To get a more precise value for F, you can make a vector diagram, drawing the 50-pound vector at the same angle to the horizontal as the pendant was when you pulled on it. Resolve this into its horizontal and vertical components. The horizontal vector is an accurate value for F for this wind velocity.

Once we know the value of F at one wind velocity, its value at other velocities can be easily calculated. F increases in proportion to the square of v. If wind speed doubles, F increases fourfold. A quadrupling of v results in an F multiplied by 16. Let us say that F in a one-knot wind is 50 pounds, and that tackle strong enough to withstand 75 knots is desired. F at 75 knots is 50 pounds $\times 75^2 = 50 \times 5,625 = 281,250$ pounds.

CYCLURA can be pulled forward by hand in a five-knot breeze. With a 27-knot wind velocity, F for CYCLURA would be 1,500 pounds; this would be the strongest wind in which she is safe on a ¾-inch nylon warp. I leave her untended only on heavy chain, which is safe up to about 45 knots. If sustained winds are expected to exceed 45 knots, I take her to sea to ride it out. An alternative is to power forward on the mooring. I have motored CYCLURA into winds up to 35 knots, so I think that full speed ahead on the mooring would cut in half the load caused by a 70-knot gale. The real danger under such conditions is the damage done by flying debris and other boats which have broken loose — the open ocean is less dangerous in a seaworthy yacht. Keep in mind that the force of the wind rises in proportion to the *square of its velocity*. Plan to protect your boat accordingly.

The force of a current on a moored boat obeys the same formula that applies to wind force. However, the values in the formula all change — some drastically. For example, water is about 825 times as dense as air (the D of our formula). This means that the drag on a body at a given velocity would be that much greater in water than in air, all other factors being equal. The underwater shape of a boat, however, is not the same as that of its topsides and superstructure; moreover, the range of current velocities is much less than the range of wind velocities. We can simply redesign our empirical test to find the current velocity that creates a 50-pound mooring load.

Tow your boat with a dinghy on a calm day and determine the maximum speed at which you can hold the tow rope in your hands without endangering life and limb. For the sake of simplicity, let us say that this limiting velocity is one knot. To calculate the load resulting from a current of five knots, multiply 50 pounds by 5^2 or 25, which gives 1,250 pounds. The conclusion to be drawn from this is clear — avoid mooring or anchoring in currents or, if this is unavoidable, as it is in the Bahamas for example, use one or more heavy tackles.

Waves that would be no cause for concern on a boat under way can be treacherous to the same boat docked or anchored. Waves communicate part of their momentum to a boat by accelerating it upwards and horizontally. This is a form of dynamic loading, and the useful point is that a boat riding waves puts dynamic loads on its ground tackle in direct proportion to its mass — heavies take note. Dynamic loading of ground tackle must be avoided as a general rule. If waves make a boat snub up, the tackle should be redesigned or a new anchorage selected.

Chain Anchor Rodes

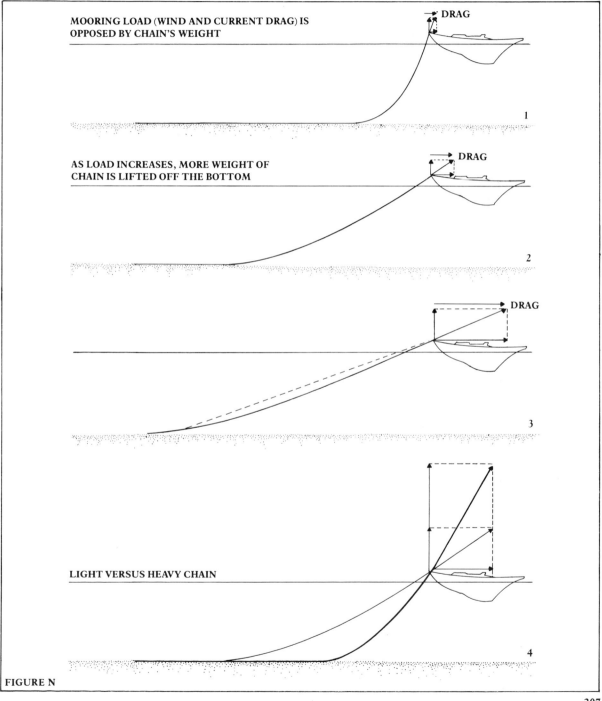

MOORING LOAD (WIND AND CURRENT DRAG) IS
OPPOSED BY CHAIN'S WEIGHT

DRAG

1

AS LOAD INCREASES, MORE WEIGHT OF
CHAIN IS LIFTED OFF THE BOTTOM

DRAG

2

DRAG

3

LIGHT VERSUS HEAVY CHAIN

4

FIGURE N

Chain, of an appropriate size and with proper gear for its handling, makes the best anchor rode due to its weight and its resistance to chafe. A widespread misconception is that chain is very strong. In fact, the breaking strength of chain and nylon rodes suitable for a given boat might not be that different (although it is reasonable to use a safety factor of about *two* for chain, giving it a considerably greater working load). Chain is weak in a very important respect: it has very low elasticity. Substantial and direct dynamic loading of chain consistently results in its failure because deceleration occurs over a very short distance, and thus generates a very large force. Many yachtsmen have sworn off chain anchor rodes after one has broken in comparatively calm conditions. What often happens is that, in calm conditions, the rode hangs almost straight down and gets tangled on some obstruction, like a coral head, as the boat drifts about. The chain is now taut in a vertical direction so that relatively small waves, accelerating the massive boat upwards, produce a dynamic load which exceeds the chain's breaking strength.

Under normal conditions, when the rode is oriented properly, the weight of chain absorbs dynamic loads. What happens is that the chain exerts a lateral load on itself, due to its weight, which acts in opposition to tension. Between the bow and the bottom, chain assumes a curved shape (called a **catenary**). Two forces act on chain at the bow of a boat: the weight of the chain, and the drag of the boat on the anchor. The weight of chain not resting on the bottom may pull the bow down some, but it is mostly opposed by the boat's buoyancy. A force vector equal and opposite to chain weight can be drawn upwards from the bow, as in figure N. The drag of the boat away from the anchor will be horizontal. Add these two vectors to find the chain tension or total load vector.

If there is very little drag, the chain will hang almost straight down, as shown in N_1. If the wind picks up, the drag will increase and the boat will move away from her anchor, lifting more of the chain from the bottom. An equilibrium is reached when the chain-tension vector is equal to the sum of the chain weight and the drag vectors, as shown in N_2. The third diagram, N_3, shows the ground tackle near the limit of its ability to hold the boat. The drag has increased until all of the chain is off the bottom and the anchor will soon break out. The anchor's holding power will be further reduced by the nearly straight rode's inability to absorb additional dynamic loads. The immediate solution to this problem would be to let out more **scope** (scope is the term for the amount of rode payed out).

All other things being equal, chain rodes need not be nearly as long as nylon rodes. With a nylon rode and a short piece of chain, scope would be at least seven times water depth, whereas with chain, three or four times water depth is usually adequate. Again, the important variable with chain is not so much the length of the rode, but its weight. Three hundred feet of chain, which is what CYCLURA carries, is enough to anchor in water 75 to 100 feet deep. If it were necessary to anchor in deeper water, a nylon rode could be shackled onto the end of the chain. The weight of chain should be as great as can be conveniently carried — CYCLURA's chain is ⅜ inch and weighs a total of 450 pounds.

Ground Tackle Design

Yachtsmen virtually never agree on ground tackle — the other yacht's gear is either inadequate or excessive. One of the causes of this confusion is that different yachtsmen depend on their ground tackle for security under quite different conditions.

The range of sizes and capacities of ground tackle is enormous. For the sake of this discussion, I will partition this spectrum into four categories: the lunch hook, the kedge, the bower, and the storm tackle.

The lunch hook is a light anchor with a short piece of chain and a nylon rode. The working loads of all components should be adequate to hold the boat under any conditions in which she would be normally used. The purpose of the lunch hook is to have an easily handled tackle to anchor for short periods when the crew will be aboard. On racers and daysailers, it may be the only ground tackle.

Many daysailers and small powerboats do not leave the dock if there is more than a 15-knot breeze; this can be considered a maximum load for the lunch hook for such boats. Medium-sized inshore cruisers generally cancel a day's sail if the wind exceeds 25 knots. This wind force can be taken as a reasonable maximum for lunch hooks in general. Boats that voluntarily operate in conditions rougher than this should have several choices of ground tackle. On CYCLURA, the lunch hook assembly consists of a Danforth 22-S anchor, 10 feet of ⅜-inch chain, and ⅞-inch nylon rode. The nylon rode is oversize so that it can also serve as a tow warp and kedge rode.

The bower is a heavier ground tackle than the lunch hook; it should be adequate to hold a boat safely when it is untended. Its load should be calculated for wind velocities up to the level of severe storms that occur less than yearly, which means a minimum of 30 knots for almost any location and as high as 50 knots in some windy regions. On CYCLURA the bower is a 45-pound CQR with a heavy swivel and 300 feet of ⅜-inch chain. It is more than adequate for the 4,500-pound load produced by a 40-knot wind. On a cruising yacht, the bower is the most frequently used ground tackle.

The kedge is traditionally a heavier anchor and rode than the bower, but it can be of the same size. In any case, it provides a backup if the bower is lost, and a second tackle when two are needed, as in two-point anchoring or kedging. CYCLURA's kedge is a 45-S Danforth and has the same chain and rode used with the lunch hook.

Storm anchors and tackles are for when all hell breaks loose. The load capacity should be calculated for winds of 100 knots or should equal one-half the boat's displacement — whichever is greater. A proper storm anchor and tackle is usually a prohibitive proposition, whether in terms of expense or accommodation; Storage space is usually at a premium on cruising yachts, which are the ones most likely to require storm gear. Two-inch line requires at least five times the storage volume as the same length of one-inch line. Some yachts carry immense storm anchors, but do not have a rode that can handle even a small fraction of its holding power.

All components of the ground tackle must be able to withstand the calculated static load with a generous safety factor. Dynamic loads are coped with in different ways. The most common method is to use a nylon rode, which is quite elastic. Selection of the appropriate diameter is critical. Dynamic

loading can extend an inadequate rode beyond its elastic limit and permanently damage it, while an oversize rode will not be elastic enough and will overload other parts of the tackle, causing failure or breaking out the anchor. Use the size of nylon line with a working load closest to your maximum calculated load. With an all-nylon rode, a length of chain, as heavy as can be handled comfortably, should separate the rode and the anchor. The chain will make the lead from the anchor more horizontal, increasing its holding power and minimizing chafe. The other important means of absorbing dynamic loads in ground tackle is weight, which opposes the tendency of the load to straighten out the rode in a line between the boat and the anchor. Chain is widely used because of its weight. It assumes a catenary shape between anchor and boat that changes with changing load. Increasing load causes some of the chain to be lifted off the bottom, absorbing the temporary increase by letting the boat move away from the anchor. When the load is reduced, the chain falls and the boat moves back toward the anchor. Because chain functions by virtue of its weight, it should be selected on this basis. Choose the heaviest chain consistent with easy handling and storage.

Gravity can also be brought into play in absorbing dynamic loads on lighter types of rodes if weights are placed or hung along the length. One device on the market makes it possible to run a weight down a nylon rode.

Ground tackle usually protects your boat and occasionally protects your life. Be careful. Calculate loads carefully. Design carefully. Assemble carefully. Inspect carefully and frequently. Be on board when it is put to its severest test.

Dock Line Loads

Wind, current, waves, opposing pull of other dock lines, people, and other boats can all apply force to dock lines. Wind does not exert substantial force on boats at rest until it gets quite strong. In a storm, the greatest threat to docked boats will usually be waves and debris, not wind. If a boat is going to weather a storm at dock, lines as strong as her ground tackle should be used, but otherwise, much smaller rope is adequate.

If there is any noticeable current, it will stress the dock lines more than normal winds. Since the simple solution of finding another dock is hardly ever available, dock lines must be able to handle this load. A current of one-half the boat's hull speed will exert a force of 10 pounds per ton of the hull's displacement. Since the working load of ½-inch nylon is more than 500 pounds, if this was all that had to be dealt with, ships of 50 tons could use dock lines of this size.

Waves generate much of the load on dock lines. The boat is accelerated in several directions by wave action, and the dock lines have to decelerate it. (Since the invention of water skis, this problem is ubiquitous.) The more elastic a dock line, the longer the distance and time over which the deceleration occurs, and the smaller the resulting force or load. A larger rope will elongate less under a given load than a smaller one, and the deceleration will occur more rapidly with the larger rope; thus the dynamic loading will be greater. This argues for small-diameter dock lines with their greater elasticity. But elasticity is an advantage only as long as the boat can travel the distance without colliding with something hard. In other words, the smaller your lines, the farther away from the dock the boat should be. It is a good idea to be as far away as possible anyway.

The opposing pull of other dock lines can be the greatest source of load. This is because tides are often ignored when boats are tied up. If the error is extreme, the boat can be left hanging from her lines at low tide. With all but the lightest boats, the lines will part and the boat will depart.

Probably the least predictable source of loads on dock lines is other yachts and their skippers. Years ago, at a yacht club to which I belonged, I docked IPHISA and left for a few hours. When I returned, another boat was tied alongside IPHISA and her spring line had been removed to make room. Both boats were hanging from IPHISA's bow line — the only line fastened to the dock which was carrying a load. Two solutions to this sort of recurring problem have occurred to me: avoid docking where others are likely to change your lines (I have quit that club), and become well known for a violent response to anyone's doing anything unauthorized to your boat.

In conclusion, I find that dock lines can be considerably smaller than what is usually recommended. Three-eighths-inch nylon is about the smallest diameter which can be easily handled, so that is the lowest limit. It is adequate on boats up to 30 feet in length. One-half-inch nylon is suitable for 40-footers like CYCLURA and five-eighths-inch for 50-footers. I have occasionally seen one-inch (i.e., oversize) dock lines on 50-foot yachts, but I have never seen dock lines which were clearly too small.

The problem with oversize dock lines is that they decelerate the boat too rapidly and increase the resulting dynamic loads. In other words, they are not elastic enough. Sometimes, elasticity has to be reduced because the boat is not clear to travel. If a short dock line is too elastic to hold the bow off a pier for example, double up the lines and leave one slightly looser. This way, the travel will be damped before it exceeds the allowable limit.

Dock Line Design

Every yacht should have an organized set of dock lines. I recommend four short pieces for bow and stern lines, and four spring lines which should be longer. The bow and stern lines should be about 25 feet long and the spring lines about 50 feet. Only rarely will all eight be used, but two can be bent together to make a long spring line and, on occasion, one will be used for some other purpose, such as lashing down the dinghy, and will not be available. Eventually, chafe will occur in dock lines, and it is good to have on hand more than the absolute minimum number.

Dock lines should all end in eye splices. The strangers who lend a hand on docks can be clearly guided as to the placement of such a line. The simple instruction to "put the eye over a cleat or piling" is hard to misunderstand. Once the eye is fixed to the dock, slack can be taken in at the deck cleat or winch. When docking single-handed, one of the short lines can be used as a breast line. With all fenders out, stop the boat alongside the dock with a dock cleat near the amidships cleat, on which the short line has been rigged. Drop the eye over the dock cleat and take up the slack. The breast line will hold her place while the other lines are rigged and adjusted. The breast line should only be used to hold the boat in place for a few minutes, as it can come under considerable loading. It can also be used as the last line cast off when getting away from a dock single-handed.

Appendix:
table of breaking strengths

Further reading
Glossary
Index

Appendix: tables of breaking strengths

		Breaking Strengths, Working Loads, and Safety Factors for Three-Strand Laid and Eight-Strand Plaited Ropes									

NYLON				POLYPROPYLENE				POLYESTER			
Diameter	New Rope Breaking Strength	Recom- mended Safety Factor	Working Load	Diameter	New Rope Breaking Strength	Recom- mended Safety Factor	Working Load	Diameter	New Rope Breaking Strength	Recom- mended Safety Factor	Working Load
Inches	Pounds		Pounds	Inches	Pounds		Pounds	Inches	Pounds		Pounds
3/16	900	12	75	3/16	720	10	72	3/16	900	10	90
1/4	1,490	12	124	1/4	1,130	10	113	1/4	1,490	10	149
5/16	2,300	12	192	5/16	1,710	10	171	5/16	2,300	10	230
3/8	3,340	12	278	3/8	2,440	10	244	3/8	3,340	10	334
7/16	4,500	11	410	7/16	3,160	9	352	7/16	4,500	9	500
1/2	5,750	11	525	1/2	3,780	9	420	1/2	5,750	9	640
9/16	7,200	10	720	9/16	4,600	8	575	9/16	7,200	8	900
5/8	9,350	10	935	5/8	5,600	8	700	5/8	9,000	8	1,130
3/4	12,800	9	1,420	3/4	7,650	7	1,090	3/4	11,300	7	1,610
13/16	15,300	9	1,700	13/16	8,900	7	1,270	13/16	14,000	7	2,000
7/8	18,000	9	2,000	7/8	10,400	7	1,490	7/8	16,200	7	2,320
1	22,600	9	2,520	1	12,600	7	1,800	1	19,800	7	2,820
1 1/16	26,000	9	2,880	1 1/16	14,400	7	2,060	1 1/16	23,000	7	3,280
1 1/8	29,800	9	3,320	1 1/8	16,500	7	2,360	1 1/8	26,600	7	3,800
1 1/4	33,800	9	3,760	1 1/4	18,900	7	2,700	1 1/4	29,800	7	4,260
1 5/16	38,800	9	4,320	1 5/16	21,200	7	3,020	1 5/16	33,800	7	4,820
1 1/2	47,800	9	5,320	1 1/2	26,800	7	3,820	1 1/2	42,200	7	6,050

Courtesy, The Cordage Institute

Breaking Strengths for Wire Cables

Nominal Diameter of Cable	Construction	Minimum Breaking Strength of Cable
Inches		Pounds
1/16	1x19	500
1/16	7x7	480
1/16	7x19	480
3/32	1x19	1,200
3/32	7x7	920
3/32	7x19	1,050
1/8	1x19	2,100
1/8	7x7	1,700
1/8	7x19	1,760
5/32	1x19	3,300
5/32	7x7	2,400
5/32	7x19	2,400
3/16	1x19	4,700
3/16	7x7	3,700
3/16	7x19	3,700
1/4	1x19	8,200
1/4	7x7	6,100
1/4	7x19	6,100
5/16	1x19	12,500
5/16	7x7	9,100
5/16	7x19	9,000
3/8	1x19	17,500
3/8	7x7	12,600
3/8	7x19	12,000

Courtesy, Loos & Co., Inc.

Breaking Strengths, Working Loads, and Weights for Chain

Chain Type	Size	Breaking Strength	Working Load	Weight per 100 feet
	Inches	Pounds	Pounds	Pounds
Proof Coil Quality	1/4	4,700	1,175	76
	5/16	7,000	1,750	115
	3/8	9,800	2,450	166
	7/16	13,000	3,250	225
	1/2	17,000	4,250	286
BBB Quality	1/4	5,300	1,325	81
	5/16	7,800	1,950	120
	3/8	11,000	2,750	173
	7/16	14,500	3,625	231
	1/2	19,000	4,750	296
Hi-Test Quality	1/4	7,750	2,500	80
	5/16	11,500	4,000	123
	3/8	16,200	5,100	175
	7/16	20,700	6,600	235
	1/2	26,000	8,200	300

Courtesy, J. Stuart Haft Co.

Glossary

ATHWARTSHIPS — Across the ship from side to side (in the direction of the thwarts).

BELAY — To make a line fast to a cleat, pin, post, or other fixed object.

BEND — Loosely, the group of knots used primarily for joining one rope or line to another.

BIGHT — A curve, loop, or bend in a length of rope.

BITTER END — The inboard end of an anchor rode.

BITTS — Short twin posts flanking the inboard end of a bowsprit.

BOLLARD — A post of iron or wood on a dock or the deck of a boat, used for making lines fast.

BREAST LINE — A dock line leading directly to a cleat abreast the vessel, without leading forward or aft.

CAM CLEAT — A device with articulated circular toothed jaws that grab and hold a line under tension.

CHAINPLATE — A fastening plate mounted on the hull of a boat by means of which the standing rigging is connected.

CHOCK — Any of various kinds of metal fittings let into gunwales or mounted on deck serving as a fairlead for dock lines, mooring lines, etc., that lead from the deck over the side.

CLEAT — A device of wood or metal with two horns fixed to deck, spar, or dock, around which ropes or lines are made fast.

CLEVIS PIN — The axle or swivel pin of a shackle or turnbuckle.

CLEW (of a sail) — The lower-aft corner of a fore-and-aft sail.

FAIR (adv.; to lead *fair*) — Straight and true; un-obstructed.

FAIR (v.) or FAIRING (n.) — To join one part of a structure with another in such a way that there is a smooth blending of external surfaces.

FAIRLEAD — A ring or other device that guides lines along a particular line, a spar or deck, or through a deck.

FID — A tool used to facilitate the interweaving of strands or other parts of rope in splicing.

GROUND TACKLE — The anchor and its associated line and tackle.

GYPSY — The drum of a windlass specially notched to fit the links of chain anchor rodes.

HANK (jib) — The hardware seized onto a jib by means of which it is attached to the headstay.

HANK (rope) — A coiled or looped bundle of rope, line, etc. To coil or loop rope or line into such a bundle.

HAWSE PIPE — Hole in a gunwale through which the anchor rode or other heavy line runs.

HEAD — The uppermost corner of a fore-and-aft sail.

HITCH — One of the group of knots whose primary function is making a rope fast to a spar, ring, stanchion, or other solid structure.

HOCKLE — A kink in a length of rope produced by twist.

LAY — Twist (as in rope).

LEAD ANGLE — The angle a line or rigging member makes with the structures it is attached to or leads through (as a block or sheave).

LINE STOPPER — A lever-operated device working by friction used to hold a line under tension.

LOAD ANGLE — The angle at which a line places a load on or absorbs a load from a structure to which it is attached or through which it passes.

LONG-JAWED — Referring to old rope that has stretched and lost much of its twist.

MEATHOOK — A projecting broken wire in a wire cable.

NIP — The place in a knot that bears severe compression.

PAINTER — Length of rope on the bow of a (small) boat used for towing or making fast.

PARTNER — A structural timber or brace.

PENDANT (mooring) — A short rope or chain, usually with a thimble spliced in one end.

PENNANT (reefing) — A short tie sewn into a sail used for reefing.

PULPIT — A platform or special railing on the bow of a boat.

RODE — Anchor line.

SAMSON POST — A sturdy square wooden post set in the bow of a boat, attached to the stem, on which lines or chains are belayed.

SCOPE — The length of rode payed out in anchoring.

SHACKLE — A U-shaped iron with a pin across the open end, used for attaching rigging members to various things such as the tacks of sails.

SHEAVE — The roller of a block. Sheaves are also used in stationary fittings. Any roller that enables a line to change direction.

SOLE (cabin) — The floor of a boat's or ship's cabin.

SPRING LINE — A line leading from the forward part of a vessel aft to the dock or from the after part forward to keep her from moving ahead or astern.

STANCHION — The upright pillars of a railing or lifeline structure.

STANDING PART (of a rope) — The inactive part as opposed to an end or bight; the part around which a knot is tied; the part that constitutes the length of rope *not* worked on — the rest of the rope.

STANDING PART (of a tackle) — The part fixed to the block or any stationary object.

STEM — The forwardmost timber or structural member of a boat, to which the sides of the bow are fixed.

STROP — A loop of rope or other material that serves as a point of fastening on a sail, spar, or block.

SURGE — To take a turn with a line around a post or cleat for the purpose of easing a load.

SWAGE — To affix a fitting or sleeve to the end of a cable or rod by means of great pressure.

TACK — The lower fore corner of a fore-and-aft sail.

TAIL (rope) — A short length of rope fastened to another rope or cable.

TAILING (to tail) — Stripping the line off the top of a winch as that line is being hauled in.

TAIL SPLICE — Splice by means of which a rope "tail" is affixed to the end of a wire-cable halyard.

TANG — Fitting by means of which rigging members are attached to spars.

TERMINAL — Toggles, forks, studs, turnbuckles, etc., attached to the ends of rigging members as fastenings or means of attachment.

TOGGLE — An articulated swivel joint in a fastening device allowing rotary motion to take place. Some joints are toggled in two axes.

TORQUE — Twisting force or force producing rotation.

TRUNION SHACKLE — A shackle incorporating a swivel or bearing.

TURNBUCKLE — A screw device used to regulate the length or tension of any assembly of rope, cable, etc. Commonly used on yachts to regulate tension in standing rigging.

TURNING BLOCK — Any stationary or fixed block whose function is to aid in changing the direction in which a line is led.

UNLAY — Untwist; take apart a twisted structure.

VANG — Tackle used to down-haul the mainsail boom.

WINCH, DIRECT-ACTION — A simple racheted winch that uses a handle to provide mechanical advantage.

WINCH, GEARED — A winch that uses internal gearing, sometimes variable, to increase mechanical advantage.

WINCH, SELF-TAILING — A winch that incorporates a device for stripping the line off the top of the drum as it is being hauled in. These winches are also self-cleating.

WINCH, SNUBBING — The simplest type of winch, consisting only of a drum racheted so that it turns in one direction only.

WINDAGE — The drag on a boat caused by friction between the air and the nondriving surfaces topsides.

WINDLASS — The winch-like device, usually using a horizontal drum or drums, whose primary function is hauling in anchors and anchor rodes. Windlasses are usually geared to produce large mechanical advantages.

Index

222

Maritime Books from David & Charles

BRITAIN'S MARITIME HERITAGE Robert Simper
222 x 146mm (8¾ x 5¾in) 8pp colour & 115 b/w photographs, 5 line drawings

BUYING A BOAT Colin Jarman
216 x 138mm (8½ x 5⅜in) 38 b/w photographs & 24 line drawings

CANADIAN PACIFIC George Musk
248 x 219mm (9¾ x 8⅝in) 90 b/w photographs & 5 maps

CHAMPIONSHIP DINGHY SAILING Christopher Caswell and David Ullman
216 x 138mm (8½ x 5⅜in) 26 b/w photographs

CORNISH SHIPWRECKS: I SLES OF SCILLY Richard Larn
216 x 138mm (8½ x 5⅜in) 33pp b/w photographs & 24 charts

DEVON SHIPWRECKS Richard Larn
216 x 138mm (8½ x 5⅜in) 32pp b/w photographs & 23 line drawings

DICTIONARY FOR YACHTSMEN Francis H. Burgess
216 x 138mm (8½ x 5⅜in) 23pp b/w photographs

FOLKLORE OF THE SEA Margaret Baker
216 x 138mm (8½ x 5⅜in) 15 b/w photographs & 9 line drawings

GLENANS WEATHER FORECASTING
187 x 124mm (7⅛ x 4⅞in) 29 b/w photographs & 82 line drawings

GOODWIN SANDS SHIPWRECKS Richard Larn
216 x 138mm (8½ x 5⅜in) 32 b/w photographs & 10 line drawings

ILLUSTRATED DICTIONARY OF NAUTICAL TERMS Graham Blackburn
230 x 152mm (9 x 6in) over 600 line drawings

IN SEARCH OF SPANISH TREASURE Sydney Wignall
234 x 156mm (9¼ x 6⅛in) 45 b/w photographs

INTRODUCTION TO DINGHY SAILING Nicolette Milnes Walker
216 x 138mm (8½ x 5⅜in) 74 line drawings

LIFEBOAT VC Ian Skidmore
216 x 138mm (8½ x 5⅜in) 19 b/w photographs & 1 line drawing

LIFEBOATS TO THE RESCUE John Beattie
216 x 138mm (8½ x 5⅜in) 26 b/w photographs & 1 map

NAVIGATION FOR OFFSHORE AND OCEAN SAILORS David Derrick
247 x 171mm (9¾ x 6¾in) 118 line drawings

NAVIGATION: An RYA Manual
247 x 171mm (9¾ x 6¾in) 4pp colour & 4 b/w photographs, 77 line drawings

NEW GLENANS SAILING MANUAL
216 x 171mm (8½ x 6¾in) 165 b/w photographs & 784 line drawings

OCEAN CROSSING WAYFARER Frank and Margaret Dye
216 x 138mm (8½ x 5⅜in) 21 b/w photographs, 14 line drawings

OPEN-BOAT CRUISING Frank and Margaret Dye
216 x 138mm (8½ x 5⅜in) 20 b/w photographs & 30 line drawings

SAILING AND BOATING: The Complete Equipment Guide Ed Colin Jarman
292 x 216mm (11½ x 8½in) 400 2-colour drawings & b/w photographs

SAILING DRIFTERS: The Story of the Herring Luggers of England, Scotland and the Isle of Man Edgar J. March
241 x 184mm (9½ x 7¼in) 78pp b/w photographs, plans & text figures

SAILING PILOTS OF THE BRISTOL CHANNEL P. J. Stuckey
216 x 138mm (8½ x 5⅜in) 28 b/w photographs & 10 line drawings

SAILING TRAWLERS Edgar J. March
241 x 184mm (9½ x 7¼in) 100pp b/w photographs, text figures & plans

SHELL COMBINED BOOK OF KNOTS AND ROPEWORK Eric C. Fry
247 x 171mm (9¾ x 6¾in) 324 b/w photographs & 11 line drawings

SHELL BOOK OF SEAMANSHIP John Russell
210 x 146mm (8¼ x 5¾in) 41 b/w photographs & 12 line drawings

SHIPWRECKS OF GREAT BRITAIN AND IRELAND Richard Larn
216 x 138mm (8½ x 5⅜in) 44 b/w photographs & 1 line drawing

SPRITSAIL BARGES OF THAMES AND MEDWAY Edgar J. March
248 x 187mm (9¾ x 7⅜in) 32pp b/w photographs, text figures & plans

STARTING SAILING James Moore and Alan Turvey
216 x 138mm (8½ x 5⅜in) 400 line drawings

TALL SHIPS ARE SAILING Holly Hollins
244 x 168mm (9⅝ x 6⅝in) 131 b/w photographs & 1 map

VOLVO PENTA AQUAMATIC BOAT ENGINE Keith Beardow
216 x 138mm (8½ x 5⅜in) 90 b/w photographs & 9 line drawings

WESTCOUNTRY SHIPWRECKS John Behenna
241 x 190mm (9½ x 7½in) 103 b/w photographs

WOODEN BOATS: Restoration and Maintenance Manual
John Scarlett
235 x 156mm (9¼ x 6⅛in) 16 b/w photographs & 203 line drawings

YACHT WIND-VANE STEERING Bill Belcher
247 x 171mm (9¾ x 6¾in) 120 line drawings

YACHTMASTER OFFSHORE: The Art of Seamanship
John Russell
216 x 138mm (8½ x 5⅜in) 12 b/w photographs & 21 line drawings

YACHTSMAN'S A-Z Henry Clarkson
210 x 146mm (8¼ x 5¾in) 345 line drawings